Addressing Vulnerability in Justice Systems

About the Advocacy Training Council and The Advocate's Gateway

The Advocacy Training Council (ATC) is established by the Council of the Inns of Court. It is responsible for providing leadership, guidance and coordination in relation to the pursuit of excellence in advocacy. The ATC comprises barristers, judges and others drawn from the Inns of Court, Circuits, the Bar Council of England and Wales, Specialist Bar Associations and other representative bodies and organisations.

The Advocate's Gateway (TAG) is designed and hosted by The Advocacy Training Council. It exists to promote excellence in the justice system's approach to vulnerable witnesses and defendants, and to develop collaboratively research-led best practice. It provides a central source of practical guidance and information for advocates and those working with witnesses and defendants with communication needs, and delivers education and training.

The Council of the Inns of Court (COIC) was established to advance education in the administration and practice of the law, and oversee and enforce professional standards of conduct in relation to the provision of advocacy and related legal services. It is an overarching body comprising senior members of the Bar and Judiciary who represent the Inns in making policy on matters referred to it by the Inns and Bar Council.

www.advocatesgateway.org

Addressing Vulnerability in Justice Systems

edited by

Professor Penny Cooper
and Linda Hunting

WS&H

Wildy, Simmonds & Hill Publishing

Copyright © The editors and authors severally 2016.

Addressing Vulnerability in Justice Systems

ISBN 9780854901968

British Library Cataloguing in Publication Data
A catalogue record for this book is available from the British Library

The right of Penny Cooper and Linda Hunting to be identified as the editors of this Work has been asserted by them in accordance with the Copyright, Designs and Patents Act 1988.

All rights reserved. No part of this book may be reproduced, stored in a retrieval system, or transmitted, in any form or by any means, electronic, mechanical, photocopying, recording or otherwise, without the consent of the copyright owners, application for which should be addressed to the publisher.

Such a written permission must also be obtained before any part of this publication is stored in a retrieval system of any nature.

This Work is published for general guidance only and is not intended as a substitute for professional advice. While every care has been taken in the preparation of the text, the publishers and authors can accept no responsibility for the consequences of any errors, however caused.

Cover Image courtesy of Paul Clark

First published in 2016 by

Published by
Wildy, Simmonds & Hill Publishing
London

For Bob and Rupert and all their support.

ACKNOWLEDGEMENTS

The Advocacy Training Council would like to thank the many individuals and organisations who have contributed to the work of The Advocate's Gateway affectionately and widely referred to as 'TAG'. We are particularly grateful to those who have given their time, been part of working groups, and shared with us their expertise in the development of toolkits. Grateful thanks to our Chair Professor Penny Cooper, Vice Chair Mr Leslie Cuthbert (SAHCA) and all of the members and organisations who are part of the Management Committee of The Advocate's Gateway. They are:, David Bartlett, Lesley Bates (CBA), Frances Edwards (CILEx), Felicity Gerry QC (Barrister, 36 Bedford Row), Dr Andy Griffiths, Elizabeth Isaacs (Barrister, St Ives Chambers), Ian Kelcey (The Law Society), Marion Langford (CPS), HHJ Patricia Lynch QC, Paul Mendelle QC (CBA), HHJ Susan Tapping, Professor Cheryl Thomas (University College London), Baljit Wirk (Ministry of Justice) David Wurtzel (Consultant Editor). Our heartfelt thanks to The Hon. Mr Justice Nicholas Green, Chair of The Advocacy Training Council for without his passion and vision for TAG our achievements since 2013 would not have been realised. We would also like to thank Wildy publishing for their support and guidance throughout the process of compiling this book. Finally, we are very grateful to The Council of the Inns of Court (COIC) and The Legal Education Foundation (LEF) whose financial support has made the development of TAG possible.

CONTENTS

Preface	xi
Introduction	xiii
The Hon. Mr Justice Green	
Avoiding Miscarriages of Justice	1
Dr. Jacqueline Wheatcroft	
Accused in International Criminal Trials: Invulnerable?	12
Dr. Andreas O'Shea	
Vulnerable Witnesses and Parties in all Civil Proceedings – Dignity, Respect and The Advocate's Gateway Toolkit 17	20
Felicity Gerry QC	
Making Special Measures Special: Reasonable Adjustments for Deaf Witnesses and Defendants	51
Dr. Sue O' Rourke & Clare Wade	
How Effective are Judges and Counsel at Facilitating Communication with Vulnerable Persons in a Criminal Trial?	69
Dr. Brendan M. O'Mahony	
Valuable Lessons and Poor Relations: Comparing the English Criminal and Family Justice Systems' Approaches to Vulnerable and Intimidated Witnesses	82
Professor Penny Cooper	
Poor Relations? Vulnerable in the Family Courts	95
Charles Geekie QC	
The Best Interests of the Accused and the Adversarial System	105
Conor Gillespie	
Putting Theory Into Practice: A Comparison of the Guidance Available to Investigative Interviewers and Advocates when using Communication Aids in the Criminal Justice System	119
Dr. Michelle Mattison	
Vulnerable Voices?	143
Jenny Talbot OBE, Waine Clegg and Anthony Fletcher	
A Postscript	150
HHJ Michael Topolski QC	

Preface

By 2012 the explosion in case law, research and new procedures merited a home on the web so I designed a blog: The Advocate's Gateway. Later that year Nick Green QC (now The Hon. Mr Justice Green), Chair of The Advocacy Training Council, readily agreed to commit resources to create a website. Neither of us could have envisaged its impact or the support the website would attract from so many quarters; academics, researchers, intermediaries, judges, lawyers, police, charities, policy makers and others have played an important part. By the time we hosted The Advocate's Gateway inaugural conference in June 2015 other jurisdictions including Australia were seeking to adopt best practice from England and Wales.

This publication, arising out of that conference, represents not only the current state of knowledge from experts in the field, but more importantly evidence of a seismic shift in the justice system. Some of the things courts and advocates did (or failed to do) now seem almost bewildering to behold. Bewildered and excluded from effective participation is how many vulnerable witnesses and defendants have felt in the courtroom. There is much more to be done, however significant progress has been made over the last decade and I am confident that this publication will play its part in keeping up that momentum.

Professor Penny Cooper
16th December 2015

Introduction

VULNERABLE WITNESSES IN COURTS - WHY?

The Hon. Mr Justice Green

I am delighted to be writing the introduction to this publication. In June 2015 the Advocacy Training Council held its Inaugural International Conference entitled *Addressing Vulnerability in Justice Systems.* This publication represents a selection of papers that were presented at the conference.

Everyone that attended the conference was in one way or another concerned with addressing vulnerability in the justice system. By way of a preface to the issues that are going to be discussed throughout this text, it is important to stand back from the fray and to seek to answer the question: Why is it important to reflect the needs of the vulnerable in a justice system?

I should like to make 8 short points.

My starting point is very basic. It is that *how* the courts treat those who are exposed and weak is a barometer of our moral worth as a society. Many of those we encounter in the criminal and family courts are from troubled backgrounds and have suffered a lifetime of disadvantage, prejudice and abuse. We should not shirk from the proposition that it is simply the right thing to do to provide an environment in which justice can be performed whilst respecting and protecting the destitute, the exposed and the weak. And we should strain every sinew to avoid the austerity measures that are being imposed on the justice system in this jurisdiction, but also elsewhere in the world, leading to a dilution in the standard of care that we afford to those who find themselves before the courts, often at a crisis moment in their lives.

The second reason is equally fundamental. It is because a justice system which relies to any degree upon an oral tradition should seek to perfect the process by which witnesses give their evidence. As such protecting the vulnerable goes the root of the quality of justice and it should be seen as a central component of a fair trial. The trial process is perfected when those giving evidence do so to the best of their ability and in the most accurate and comprehensive way possible and this is so quite irrespective of which side of the trial divide they are on. It matters not whether the witness is a defendant, a complainant or victim or a third party. Those who suffer from vulnerability are or may be inhibited in giving of their best. They may be overwhelmed by the court process. They might not understand or they might be confused by the questions posed to them but be unwilling or scared to seek clarification. They might be in awe of and cowed by the authority figure before them (advocate and/or judge) and simply submit and agree, regardless of whether this is the truth or the whole truth. When this happens truth is compromised and justice is weakened. It is for these reasons that in cases involving vulnerable persons we need to adapt our normal rules and procedures and for example adapt the usual questioning techniques.

A third reason why the justice system must protect the vulnerable is because the "legitimacy" of the system depends in large measure upon the confidence reposed in it by the public and the public in recent years has shown itself deeply concerned at the plight of two particular categories of person: female victims of sex crimes and physical abuse, and children subject to physical or sexual abuse by adults. The media is replete with accounts of the traumas suffered by woman and children as victims of crime and the interest of the public is whetted by these tragedies as they are recalled and unpicked in courts of law. In this digital era of instant communication what happens in a court room can be, and is, relayed across the world almost simultaneously. A victim giving evidence who appears to be subject to oppressive questioning or unfair treatment by a judge can trigger a more or less instantaneous adverse reaction in the world outside. An unguarded observation made by a judge or prosecution advocate – both of whom should know better in the eyes of the public – becomes headline news. Journalists sit in cases tweeting and twittering and so in a real sense the eyes of the public are upon us; judging us at the same time as we judge others. Recognising this and ensuring that we both understand different vulnerabilities and respond to them appropriately is accordingly essential. It ensures the maintenance of confidence amongst society at large and if we lose this confidence we risk doing lasting damage to the rule of law.

Fourth, addressing vulnerability is also about recognising diversity and gender. We all know that in sex and domestic violence cases complainants are invariably female and are routinely scared of cooperating with the police and do not complain, and even if they do at first cooperate they frequently then retract their evidence either because of pressures from family or from the wider community that they come from or out of fear of reprisals. As lawyers and others involved in the justice system our ability to protect the vulnerable can go some way to recognising and responding to the particular problems that such woman and those from diverse ethnic backgrounds confront.

The fifth point I wish to make is that the impetus for change and for development in our practices in this area must come not from central government but from within; from practising judges and lawyers and other working day by day in the system. We are the experts. I simply do not accept that Government has the skill or expertise to find real solutions. For instance it has to be practitioners who are familiar with the nuanced dynamics of courts procedures who can work out precisely what sorts of questions are appropriate and what are not. Practitioners who are experienced in the relevant techniques know that in many cases there may be no sure-fire right and wrong answers. A huge dollop of judgment is frequently called for by all the parties to a case which takes account of the specific degree of vulnerability of the actual witness in question. Everyone is different and individual differences need to be responded to. In this jurisdiction the work of the Advocacy Training Council has been conducted by an amalgam of those who truly know what they are doing. It includes experts from the Bar and from the solicitor's profession, judges trying sex and family cases, leading academics, children's charities, intermediaries, expert prosecutors and others who set the standards. There is no room in our work for political hay making or posturing. The job is to do what needs to be done, no more and no less. To date Government has recognised this and has been content to follow our lead and has provided support and encouragement. We must therefore continue to lead from the front. If we do not then such is the potential for real and genuine concern being expressed amongst the public that the politicians *will* feel inclined or pressurised to step in. Protecting the vulnerable in the justice system is one of those issues that will attract that eponymous press headline "something needs to be done". So do it we should and indeed do it we must.

The sixth point is that recognising vulnerability is not just a matter of adapting procedures used in court rooms it is also an issue of substantive law and rules of evidence. Thus far we have concentrated in our work on what might be called the obvious targets: special measures; types of questions, etc. But as thinking evolves in relation to vulnerability I believe that we will identify a wider variety of areas where adaptation is required. So by way of example if a vulnerable person refuses to give evidence for a reason connected to that vulnerability then that should, in principle, be a factor taken into account in deciding upon the operation of the hearsay rule of admissibility, for instance permitting statements to be read or alternative pieces of evidence being admitted to substantiate the case that the vulnerable person is truly a victim. In this context I noted with interest the judgment of the Divisional Court in *Barnaby v DPP* [2015] EWHC 232

(6th February 2015). There the charge against the Defendant was domestic abuse. The wife did not give evidence because of fear of reprisals. She was in this sense vulnerable. She was not summonsed to give evidence. The magistrates admitted however transcripts of three emergency 999 calls to the police and other extraneous evidence as part of the *res gestae*. A case stated was sent to the Divisional Court challenging the admission of this evidence. The Court held that the Magistrates acted lawfully. Without casting their judgment in terms of vulnerability or as a response to the needs of a vulnerable witness the Court nonetheless used the exposed and hence vulnerable position of the complainant as the reason to justify the admission of the disputed evidence. Lord Justice Fulford at paragraph [34] stated this:

> Although the court has a cardinal responsibility to ensure that a defendant receives a fair trial, careful decisions need to be taken in situations of this kind if there is a real risk that a victim of domestic abuse may suffer further harm following her cooperation with the prosecuting authorities.
>
> Here, the prosecution was aware from the outset that Ms Gibb was frightened that providing a witness statement might provoke a violent reaction from the appellant. This was not a situation in which the prosecution was seeking to resort to unfair tactics in order to avoid introducing evidence that was potentially inconsistent with the case against the defendant, or because it simply anticipated that there was a risk the witness might give an untruthful account. The Crown's stance was a seemingly sensible recognition of the potentially dangerous position in which Ms Gibb had been placed.
>
> Given these facts, it was appropriate to admit this res gestae evidence notwithstanding, in a strict sense, Ms Gibb was available as a witness, for instance if the court had issued a witness summons.

The case is interesting for no reason other than it is unremarkable. All that I derive from this is that in cases of vulnerability it is important that we do not become overly focused upon procedural issues but we also consider how the fact of vulnerability can also be a significant consideration in substantive decision such as in the exercise of discretion to admit or exclude evidence.

My seventh observation looks to the future. It is only recently that we have, in any systematic way, begun to focus upon how issues of vulnerability interact with the justice system. In the future we must do two things in particular. First we must extend this new learning into new areas of practice. Our starting point, perhaps naturally enough, has been in the field of crime. But we are moving rapidly outwards into family law and from there we need to identify all other areas where similar issues arise, such as immigration and asylum. The second thing we must do is spread our learning backwards into the hinterland of court proceedings. So, in the context of crime for instance, we must work with the police and the Crown Prosecution Service and with those in the social services and in charities who deal with the vulnerable *before* they come to court. A person is vulnerable not just in the court room but at all of the stages leading up to trial. The considerations identified above can apply equally at these earlier points in time. An obvious example is the complainant who gives evidence during an Achieving Best Evidence interview shortly after the alleged crime which is then to stand as evidence in chief at trial. If there needs to be control of questioning in court by advocates then the same should apply to the questions posed by the police during the earlier interview.

My eighth and final point concerns transparency. Vulnerability is a human characteristic and it knows no international boundaries. As such the work being conducted in one jurisdiction can inform the work being performed in this area elsewhere. The Advocacy Training Council through its internet portal - The Advocates Gateway ("TAG") - has endeavoured to create a transparent, neutral and open platform. The material that is being placed upon TAG, in the form of "toolkits" and other guidance material, is available to the world at large. TAG has since its inception become embedded in the procedural culture of this jurisdiction. Practitioners are now required to have resort to the material contained on the site. But an important objective of TAG is also to stimulate an international debate. We would be only too pleased if our materials were adopted in other jurisdictions and then the fruits of the research and experience of other lawyers elsewhere in the world was fed back to us so that we could take it on board and improve the material we work with. Even better would be the creation of a series of world-wide TAGs acting a network of focal points for the debate.

In short we are on a steep learning curve. We should assume that it will take time to reach the top of the curve and we need to maintain an open mind and be prepared to change our practices and our techniques as learning evolves. And if we do this we will make lasting improvements to the justice system.

The work of advocates and others in justice systems is indispensable to the effective work of the courts and therefore to the administration of justice and the rule of law. This collection of papers offers profound insights into this crucial area of work and it can unquestionably progress our collecting thinking on the subject.

I would offer my congratulations to all those who contributed to the conference and to the staff of the Advocacy Training Council and the Management Committee of The Advocate's Gateway who in conjunction with the publishers have produced this publication.

The Hon. Mr Justice Nicholas Green
The Royal Courts of Justice, December 2015

Avoiding Miscarriages of Justice

DR. JACQUELINE WHEATCROFT
University of Liverpool
Chartered and Registered Practitioner Forensic Psychologist
Co-Chair British Psychological Society Division of Forensic Psychology TC

INTRODUCTION

In 1998 the Home Office for England and Wales produced the 'Speaking up for Justice Initiative' which attempted to make the criminal justice system more victim-centred with an emphasis on facilitating the gaining and giving of evidence through safeguarding witnesses at all stages of proceedings (e.g., Achieving Best Evidence and use of Special Measures[1]). Techniques had already been pioneered with children and 78 recommendations made[2]. Vulnerable groups however are still overrepresented as victims of crime, underrepresented in court, and there remain problems in collecting evidence because of communication difficulties despite the use of intermediaries and other associated measures.[3] Those who are intimidated and fear the process and confronting the accused suffer additional difficulties in coping with the traditional features of adversarial systems of justice, such as cross-examination.[4]

Whilst much improvement has been seen in how the police obtain best information from witness interviews[5] and the introduction of the Domestic

---

[1] *Achieving Best Evidence in Criminal Proceedings: Guidance on interviewing victims and witnesses, and guidance on using special measures* (2011) London: Home Office.
[2] Mandy Burton, Roger Evans and Andrew Sanders, 'Are Special Measures for Vulnerable and Intimidated Witnesses Working? Evidence from the Criminal Justice Agencies', Home Office Online Report 01/06. Summarised in Burton, M, Evans, R and Sanders, A (2006) An evaluation of the use of special measures for vulnerable and intimidated witnesses, *Home Office Research Findings 270*
[3] *See* http://www.advocacytrainingcouncil.org/vulnerable-witnesses/advocates-gateway for a detailed consideration of practical, evidence-based guidance on vulnerable witnesses and defendants.
[4] *See* Jacqueline M. Wheatcroft, Graham Wagstaff & Annmarie Moran, 'Re-Victimising the Victim? How rape victims experience the UK legal system', 4 (2009) *Victims and Offenders* 265.
[5] Jacqueline M. Wheatcroft and Graham Wagstaff, 'An example of a Solution-Focused Academic-Practitioner Co-operation: How the iIIRG facilitated the development of the Liverpool Interview Protocol' (2014), 6(1) *Investigative Interviewing: Research and Practice*, 42-50.

Violence, Crime & Victims Act (2004)[6], witnesses, despite much progress in regard to use of special measures, continue to suffer impediments in process. The Act may be missing many witnesses who are in need of assistance. Work conducted on examination in court suggests that many, even experts with experience of giving evidence and being subject to cross-examination, struggle with this feature of the process.[7] Thus all lay witnesses are particularly vulnerable and those classified as vulnerable are especially susceptible. For example, research interviews conducted with rape victim witnesses found a number of themes emerged; one was court re-victimisation. One participant Sally (anonymised) reflected on her courtroom experience and gave a brief account of how she felt about the in court process and how it had affected her. She notes:

> I had to sit in front of the man who raped me and tell loads of strangers what he did to me. They exhibited my underwear, talked about my body, and called me a liar. They showed intimate pictures of my body, you know injuries and stuff, and I felt violated all over again. The defence just seemed to want to break me. They raped me again. I felt so ashamed. I was on trial, not him. I went there as a liar to try and prove what I was saying was the truth. I had to account for every aspect of my life.[8]

Whereas this report represents a single example it does appear to mirror repeated discussions in research works[9] and commentaries in some media reports.[10]

In adversarial systems considerable faith continues to be placed in the capacity of cross-examination to expose flaws, errors and contradictions in witness testimony.[11] Such a contention awaits empirical examination.

---

[6] Domestic Violence, Crime and Victims Act 2004 (c 28) see UK Legislation at http://www.legislation.gov.uk/ukpga/2004/28

[7] Gisli Gudjonsson, 'Psychologists as expert witnesses: The 2007 BPS Survey', (2007) 92 *Forensic Update* 23; Gisli Gudjonsson, 'Psychological evidence in court: Results from the BPS survey' (1995) 383 *Bulletin of the British Psychological Society* 327; Gisli Gudjonsson, 'Psychological evidence in court: Results from the 1995 survey' 52 *The Psychologist* 213.

[8] Jacqueline M. Wheatcroft, Graham Wagstaff & Annmarie Moran, 'Re-Victimising the Victim? How rape victims experience the UK legal system', (2009) 4 *Victims and Offenders*, 247

[9] *See* Jacqueline M. Wheatcroft, Graham Wagstaff & Annmarie Moran, 'Re-Victimising the Victim? How rape victims experience the UK legal system', (2009) 4 *Victims and Offenders*, 265; Louise Ellison, 'Witness preparation and the prosecution of rape', (2007) 27 *Legal Studies*, 171; Jacqueline M. Wheatcroft and Sandra Walklate (2014) 'Thinking differently about 'False Allegations' in cases of rape: The search for truth', 3 *International Journal of Criminology & Sociology*, 239.

[10] See http://www.channel4.com/news/cross-examinations-too-harsh-for-rape-victims-says-labour

[11] Marcus Stone, *Cross-examination in Criminal Trials, 3rd Edn (2009)*, Haywards Heath: Tottel Publishing; Louise Ellison and Jacqueline Wheatcroft, 'Exploring the influence of courtroom questioning and pre-trial preparation on adult witness accuracy' (2010) *Research Briefing*

However, a girl aged nine who faced aggressive cross-examination says she has never recovered. Describing her experience of being cross-examined over video link in a side room of the court, she stated:

> They took me to a tiny room with a TV screen. It wasn't like a front room it was very cold and blank. There was a lady I hadn't met before and one I'd met once. I didn't really know who they were. When I started to get upset, I was allowed to sit outside the room for five minutes and sit in a corridor on some chairs. The women comforted me, but not really.[12]

In another case Frances Andrade, a talented violinist, took her own life after being called a liar and a fantasist in court by the barrister (Manchester, England). It was reported the overdose was a way of the witness coping with the trial.[13] Such cases illustrate the in court process as very stressful for witnesses and highlights the need for the development and maintenance of *effective* support, particularly with the process of assisting witnesses in the giving of their best evidence. It is proposed the criminal justice system might have both high and unreasonable expectations of witnesses as the examples shown suggest witnesses do not always cope sufficiently with processes without effective support.

It is of utmost importance therefore that the equilibrium between testing witness veracity and obtaining accurate reports from the witness is maintained. Accordingly, the pre-trial process needs to ensure that witnesses are aware of what is expected of them in the courtroom; that is, that they be given information about the procedure, be offered the opportunity to ask questions, and be placed at ease. Indeed, the significance of clear guidelines to encourage accurate testimony in court seems essential, particularly given some commentators note 'the kinds of questions asked in cross-examination are subject to very little regulation', and that 'trial judges should generally ensure that questions are relevant and courteously put, but seem unable to protect some witnesses from being hectored or humiliated'.[14] Research suggests that certain question types are damaging to witness evidence.

Paper produced for the Arts & Humanities Research Council (AHRC), Universities of Leeds and Liverpool.
[12] *See* http://www.independent.co.uk/news/uk/crime/court-is-just-as-traumatic-girl-who-faced-aggressive-crossexamination-aged-nine-says-she-has-never-recovered-8631662.html; accessed 29th May 2015.
[13] See http://www.bbc.co.uk/news/uk-england-28489500; accessed 29th May 2015.
[14] J. McEwan, 'Special measures for witnesses and victims' (2002) M. McConville, G. Wilson, *The Handbook of the Criminal Justice Process*, pp. 237-251. (Oxford University Press: Oxford, 2002) 248

THE IMPACT OF QUESTIONING

As noted earlier, cross-examination procedures have been considered by the legal profession to be crucial for probing the accuracy of evidence obtained in examination-in-chief, and to expose unreliable or dishonest witnesses. Hickey notes cross-examination is "a legitimate, effective and perfectly respectable contribution to the judicial process" and "performs a crucial function in the objectives of witness information and witness credibility".[15] However, a growing body of evidence shows that commonly employed questioning techniques render the procedure of cross-examination a daunting one for most witnesses and represent an unusual situation that can cause sufficient discomfort and stress to impact and undermine the recall accuracy and completeness, and beyond.[16] Court observation, analysis of trial transcripts and research have, for example, revealed how witnesses are commonly confronted with complex questions containing multiple parts, negatives, double-negatives and advanced vocabulary and/or legal terminology.[17] Unsurprisingly then the studies indicate that these kinds of questions can be difficult to decipher and respond to with accuracy.[18] Moreover, some argue that cross-examination is used as a tool to humiliate, intimidate and confuse opposing witnesses. The use of intrusive attacks made on the character and general credibility of witnesses can cause extreme distress while threatening to distort the fact-finding process.[19] One way of challenging witness evidence is by the use of leading questions. These questions, which contain pre-suppositional statements, often seek a 'yes' or 'no' response and have likewise been shown to have an adverse influence on accuracy when compared to more open questioning strategies.[20] Leading questions are, by definition, suggestive

---

[15] Leo Hickey, 'Presupposition under Cross-Examination' (1993) 1(16) *International Journal for the Semiotics of Law* 89 (see 109 and 99 respectively).

[16] *See for summary* Jacqueline M. Wheatcroft, David Caruso and James Krumrey-Quinn, 'Rethinking Leading: The Directive, Non-Directive Divide', (2015) 5 *Crim. L.R.* 340; and Emily Henderson '"Did you see the broken headlight?" Questioning the cross-examination of robust adult witnesses' 10 *Archbold Rev*iew (2014) 4.

[17] Jacqueline M. Wheatcroft & Louise Ellison 'Evidence in Court: Witness preparation and cross-examination style effects on adult witness accuracy' (2012) 30 *Behavioral Sciences & the Law*, 821.

[18] Janet Cotterill, *Language and Power in Court* (2003), New York: Palgrave MacMillan; D. Dodd and J. Bradshaw, J. 'Leading Questions and Memory: Pragmatic Constraints' (1980) 19 *Journal of Verbal Learning and Verbal Behavior* 695; Mark Kebbell and D. Giles. 'Lawyers' questions and witness confidence: Some experimental influences of complicated lawyers' questions on witness confidence and accuracy' (2000) 134 *The Journal of Psychology* 129.

[19] S. Caroline Taylor, *Court licensed abuse: Patriarchal lore and the legal response to intra-familial sexual abuse of children* (2004) New York: Peter Lang Publishing.

[20] Jacqueline M. Wheatcroft, Graham Wagstaff and Mark Kebbell, 'The influence of courtroom questioning style on actual and perceived eyewitness confidence and accuracy' (2004) 9 *Legal & Criminological Psychology*, 8-101

(for example, 'The car was red, wasn't it?') and aim to limit responses made to a two-alternative forced choice (i.e. yes/no), and elicit preferred answers in the context of 'yeah'[21] (i.e., consistent passive 'yes' responses). As such concerns have been raised in that certain questions can suggest or even compel responses and interfere with the fairness of the process.

Nevertheless, a feature of advocacy tuition is leading.[22] Its use is argued necessary to comply with certain rules of evidence, for example, as specified in *Browne v Dunn*.[23] The form is taboo in examination-in-chief and the leading question itself has, however, received little scrutiny.[24] Its definition however, as developed at common law, focuses on the content of the question, failing to account for the significant impact of its form on the witness. Legal definitions do not differentiate between the different forms leading may take, primarily, directive and non-directive, and their effect on witness reports.

Wheatcroft and Woods[25] made this distinction and examined the effects directive forms had upon witness accuracy. The study revealed that when directive leading was compared against non-directive counterparts, adult witnesses were significantly less accurate in response to directive form; the form alone produced that result.[26] It can be expected therefore that when directive leading questions are incorporated into the cross-examination procedure a witness's overall accuracy will be reduced. The researchers also discussed how the distinction might more usefully define the question form appropriate for use in cross-examination, in that there should be no place for questions that sideline the search for fact in the trial process.[27] At the very least, there should be no place for questions that impact negatively upon witness accuracy.

---

[21] Sandra Harris, 'Questions as a mode of control in magistrates' courts' (1984) 49 *International Journal of Society and Language* 5-27.
[22] *See, eg,* Iain Morley, *The Devil's Advocate*, 2nd edn (2009), pp. 158–9; Thomas A. Mauet & Les A McCrimmon, *Fundamentals of Trial Technique*, 3rd edn (2011), pp. 199–200 and Peter Murphy, *Evidence and advocacy, 4th edn (1994)* London: Blackstone Press.
[23] *Browne v Dunn* (1893) 6 R. 67 (House of Lords): a cross-examiner must put the nature of his case in full to the witness in cross-examination, to give him or her the opportunity to comment on or explain the contradictory version.
[24] *But see* Jacqueline M. Wheatcroft, David Caruso and James Krumrey-Quinn, 'Rethinking Leading: The Directive, Non-Directive Divide', (2015) 5 *Crim. L.R.* 340; Adrian Keane & Rudi Fortson, 'Leading Questions: A Critical Analysis' (2011) 4 *Crim.L.R.* 280.
[25] Jacqueline M. Wheatcroft and Sarah Woods 'Effectiveness of witness preparation and cross-examination non-directive leading and directive leading question styles on witness accuracy and confidence' (2010) 14(3) *International Journal of Evidence & Proof,* 189.
[26] Jacqueline M. Wheatcroft, David Caruso and James Krumrey-Quinn, 'Rethinking Leading: The Directive, Non-Directive Divide', (2015) 5 *Crim. L.R.* 340; Adrian Keane & Rudi Fortson, 'Leading Questions: A Critical Analysis' (2011) 4 *Crim.L.R.* 280.
[27] *See* Mark Brennan, 'The Discourse of Denial: CrossExamining Child Victim Witnesses' (1995) 23 Journal of Pragmatics 71.

Avoiding Miscarriages of Justice

Given the pressures placed upon witnesses and a suggestion that guidelines meant to highlight the vulnerability of victims and special measures, such as allowing evidence to be given behind screens, "are not having their intended effect"[28] what approaches are at the courts disposal to ensure witnesses are assisted in giving their best evidence? One which has been considered useful is of preparing witnesses to the process of giving evidence.

WITNESS FAMILIARISATION

One key aim of witness familiarisation is to identify standard tactics used by lawyers in the course of cross-examination and to provide witnesses with practical advice on how best to approach the interaction on the assumption that preparation will assist witnesses to give more complete and accurate evidence. Put simply, courtroom procedures should be designed to optimise witness accuracy and if witnesses can be prepared and supported in ways that help them with daunting cross-examination which leads to effective performance in court then their use would be most valuable. Confidence that the aim of the trial can be realised would be increased. However it is important to recognise the value of witness experience and how to maximise witness reports of the same. According to a Home Office witness survey levels of satisfaction for categories of witnesses involved in the courtroom process varied greatly. Prosecution witnesses (68 per cent), especially victims, were less satisfied with the defence lawyer (48 per cent) than defence witnesses (90 per cent). The marked reduced effects on satisfaction ratings were observed more keenly in oppositional exchanges, with the largest variation shown for victim witness transactions with the defence. Such findings illustrate greater levels of support for all witnesses in coping with oppositional interactions when testifying are needed.

The courts have endorsed the practice of witness familiarisation approving the right of barristers to prepare witnesses on conduct appropriate to the courtroom and more specifically how to give effective evidence. In *Salisbury*, the trial judge, Mr Justice Pitchford, heard that the preparation had been delivered by a Bar member, and stated that there was a "difference of substance" between orchestrated evidence and familiarisation to giving evidence coherently, stating:

---

[28] *See* http://www.independent.co.uk/news/uk/crime/court-guidelines-for-rape-victims-are-not-working-as-study-finds-aggressive-crossexamination-and-intimidating-encounters-are-still-common-10031451.html.

...This, it seems to me, was an exercise any witness should be entitled to enjoy. What was taking place was no more than preparation for the exercise of giving evidence.

Similarly, in *Momodou* the Court of Appeal (Judge LJ) held that witnesses should not be disadvantaged by ignorance of the process, nor when they come to give evidence, taken by surprise at the way it works, and that:

...Sensible preparation for the experience of giving evidence, which assist the witness to give of his or her best at the forthcoming trial, is permissible ... The process may improve the manner in which the witness gives evidence by, for example, reducing the nervous tension arising from inexperience of the process.[29]

Witnesses can be informed about the basic rationale of cross-examination (to discredit opposing testimony) and directed to listen carefully to questions, to request clarification where appropriate and never to answer a question they do not understand. Wheatcroft and Ellison conducted the first RCUK funded research into the effectiveness of witness familiarisation. The researchers manipulated complex and simple vocabulary used in cross-examination with witnesses who had been familiarised and those who had not received any preparation to the process. Overall, the findings showed witnesses who had been familiarised were more accurate, made fewer errors, and made increased requests for clarification; lending support to those who suggest witness preparation is essential for the improvement of witness evidence in court.

It is interesting to reflect upon why familiarisation might be helpful. A number of explanations have been put forward drawn from the psychological literature.[30] More complex tasks, such as answering lawyerly cross-examination questions, require greater cognitive effort and thereby activate executive and frontal systems with potential to lead to fewer correct responses as a result of lowered processing capacity. Inhibition of correct responses may also be influenced by witnesses drawing upon cognitive coping methods, such as those defaults to more autonomic responses that require little in the way of cognitive work, yet result in lower accuracy. In the complex context of the courtroom, mental shortcuts, which can often help to streamline information in daily activities, can become detrimental resulting in a greater number of errors.

---

[29] *R v Momodou* [2005] 1 W.L.R. 3442; *R v Salisbury* [2005] EWCA Crim 3107.

[30] Graham Wagstaff, Jacqueline M. Wheatcroft, et al., 'Some cognitive and neuropsychological aspects of social inhibition and facilitation' (2007) *European Journal of Cognitive Psychology*, 20(4), 828-846; Jacqueline M. Wheatcroft and Louise Ellison, 'Evidence in Court: Witness preparation and cross-examination style effects on adult witness accuracy', (2012) *Behavioral Sciences & the Law*, 30, 821-840.

The prior exposure to techniques used in cross-examination in court appears to allow witnesses to organize knowledge of events such that information may be accessed more readily in response to lawyerly questions. Thus, the guidance appears to allow for some method of 'updating' to occur making accessible the information for use as and when appropriate. Further, familiarization with the questioning techniques seems to 'free up' capacity in the brain to process information, but if a witness is not given guidance the frontal–executive brain systems are potentially forced to work harder, leaving less processing capacity to work on the process of comprehending, understanding, formulating, and responding to questions. It remains for research to consider whether questioning will make the effects of delay more problematic.[31]

Conversely, witnesses who are not given prior guidance are likely to work much harder to answer cross-examination questions accurately and may tend, in addition, to become nervous and frustrated in court.

Witness familiarisation approaches evidenced herein appear to show some promise. In addition, there is fresh ground covered in regard to the questioning put to those classed as vulnerable in the form of what has become termed Ground Rules Hearings. These are commonly used by judges to set the parameters for the fair treatment of vulnerable defendants and vulnerable witnesses.[32]

GROUND RULES HEARINGS AND QUESTIONING

In 2013 Ground Rules Hearings (GRHs) were recognised by the Criminal Practice Directions[33] (CPD) as a key step in planning the proper questioning of a vulnerable[34] witness or defendant.[35] Professsor Penny Cooper and her colleagues have examined the evolution of practice and law, including restrictions on 'putting your case' to a vulnerable witness, using an illustrative case example. The authors concluded from their analysis that a checklist for GRHs to support the development of best practice would be an entirely reasonable step to take.[36] Such a standardised move would ensure

---

[31] Jacqueline M. Wheatcroft, Graham Wagstaff and Brian Manarin, 'The influence of delay and item difficulty on eyewitness confidence and accuracy' (2015) 1 *International Journal of Humanities and Social Science Research*.

[32] Cooper, Penny, Backen, Paula and Marchant, Ruth (2015) Getting to grips with Ground Rules Hearings – a checklist for judges, advocates and intermediaries, *Criminal Law Review*, 2015, 6, 417-432.

[33] Criminal Practice Directions [2013] EWCA Crim 1631 in particular at '3E: Ground Rules Hearings to plan the questioning of a vulnerable witness or defendant'

[34] Penny Cooper (2014) 'Ticketing Talk Gets Serious', *Counsel*, November 11-12

[35] Emily Henderson (2014) 'Jewel in the Crown?', *Counsel*, November 10-12

[36] Cooper, Penny, Backen, Paula and Marchant, Ruth (2015) Getting to grips with Ground Rules Hearings – a checklist for judges, advocates and intermediaries, *Criminal Law Review*,

greater consistency in application and afford greater levels of protections. In respect of GRHs specifically, in England and Wales there have been three cases (i.e., *Dixon*[37]; *Re A (A Child) (Vulnerable Witness)* [38]; *and Lubemba*[39]). In the latter the Court of Appeal heard two cases together because each raised a similar issue which surrounded the question of what measures a judge might be able to take to protect vulnerable witnesses without impacting on the accused right to a fair trial. It was noted by the Vice President:

> …judges are taught, in accordance with the Criminal Practice Directions, that it is best practice to hold hearings in advance of the trial to ensure the smooth running of the trial, to give any special measures directions and to set the ground rules for the treatment of a vulnerable witness. We would expect a ground rules hearing in every case involving a vulnerable witness, save in very exceptional circumstances. If there are any doubts on how to proceed, guidance should be sought from those who have the responsibility for looking after the witness and or an expert.[40]

Furthermore, in *Lubemba* the trial judge's *duty* was emphasised, particularly in respect of the questioning process:

> As we have already explained, a trial judge is not only entitled, he is duty bound to control the questioning of a witness. He is not obliged to allow a defence advocate to put their case. He is entitled to and should set reasonable time limits and to interrupt where he considers questioning is inappropriate.[41]

Lubemba suggests there is no right to put a case to a witness, in this case, a child. Indeed, leading questions may not even be a suitable and proper means of challenging the account of a 'robust' adult witness[42] either.

While witness familiarisation shows promise for all witnesses and GRHs for those classed as vulnerable we must ask, are these the best remedies to enable witnesses to give of their best evidence? Should witnesses be left to deal with the shortcomings of the system? Is it right and proper that witnesses who may be able to enable their wit or have increased ability to

---

2015, 6, 417 -432
[37] *R v Dixon* [2013] EWCA Crim 465
[38] *Re A (A Child) (Vulnerable Witness)* [2013] EWHC 1694
[39] *R v Lubemba; R v JP* [2014] EWCA Crim 2064, conjoined appeals
[40] Ibid, para 42
[41] *R v Lubemba* [2014] EWCA Crim 2064, para 51
[42] Cooper, Penny, Backen, Paula and Marchant, Ruth (2015) Getting to grips with Ground Rules Hearings – a checklist for judges, advocates and intermediaries, *Criminal Law Review*, 2015, 6, 417-432.

cope with pressures be allowed to operate in conditions that mean they will be more successful in their testimony than those who cannot?

REFORM CROSS-EXAMINATION: PROHIBIT DIRECTIVE LEADING

The mechanism of cross-examination is designed to break down dubious testimony, and if it does then this is to be applauded. However, as early as 1939, it was shown that witness testimony reliability dropped when witnesses answered questions applied during cross-examination.[43] However, as noted earlier, putting leading, and only leading, questions is a hallmark of advocacy tuition in cross-examination as they comply with certain rules of evidence.[44] That is to say, the defence lawyer must challenge the truthfulness of the complainant. Despite its centrality, the leading question has received little judicial, legislative or academic attention.[45]

It is argued that the current approach to the leading question does not assist or promote the accuracy of witness evidence. Given the psychological evidence base one cannot help but ask if the measures noted merely dampen the known consequences of certain examination techniques rather than dealing directly with the mischief in cross-examination. There is appetite for change which is personified in *Lubemba*. A direct change that will bring about immediate effect is to prohibit the directive leading question leaving in place the less likely to confuse counterpart, the non-directive leading form.

CONCLUSION

The need for change has created conditions where new approaches to assist witnesses in giving of their best evidence have been developed. Witness familiarisation and ground rules hearings represent two of these developments which have shown promise in the facilitation of witness evidence in court. However, these are in infancy. Research has shown that permissibility of directive leading questions during cross-examination in court is warranted and provides an immediate solution to prohibit some negative aspects of the cross-examination process together with

---

[43] William Stern, 'The psychology of testimony' (1939) 34(1) Journal of Abnormal and Social Psychology 3

[44] *Browne v Dunn* (1893) 6 R. 67 (House of Lords): a cross-examiner must put the nature of his case in full to the witness in cross-examination, to give him or her the opportunity to comment on or explain the contradictory version.

[45] Jacqueline M. Wheatcroft, David Caruso and James Krumrey-Quinn, 'Rethinking Leading: The Directive, Non-Directive Divide', (2015) 5 Crim. L.R. 340

the opportunity to enhance other features of the way advocates test oral evidence in the 21st century of adversarial litigation.[46]

---

[46] Jacqueline M. Wheatcroft, David Caruso and James Krumrey-Quinn, 'Rethinking Leading: The Directive, Non-Directive Divide', (2015) 5 Crim. L.R. 340

Accused in International Criminal Trials: Invulnerable?

DR. ANDREAS O'SHEA
Barrister

INTRODUCTION

National courts have developed principles for addressing the vulnerability of defendants. In the UK this is reflected in *Criminal Practice Direction (General matters) 3G*, October 7 2013 and in case law[1].

The development of international criminal procedure is in its infancy compared to national proceedings. In the UK measures to alleviate the situation of vulnerable adult defendants was inspired by the European Court of Human Rights approach to young defendants.[2].

In the international arena, children are not tried. While the Special Court for Sierra Leone has jurisdiction over persons aged between 15 and 18,[3] this has not been exercised. The issue of young persons' vulnerability has been the reserve of witness protection, particularly for child soldiers.[4]

Yet adult defendants in international proceedings can be the victims of trauma. Deaths in detention have occurred. Consider the situations of Robert Ley and Hermann Göring at the Nuremberg trial, and in more modern times, Milosevic and Nzirorera. In the case of Seselj, it might be suspected that the fear of his death led to decisions in his favour. Andre Rwamakuba stayed away from his two trials before the International Criminal Tribunal for Rwanda completely[5] (and was acquitted).

This paper questions whether such accused leaders could be vulnerable and what measures might be appropriate.

---

[1] See *R v H* (2006) 150 SJ CA
[2] See *T v UK*; *V v UK*, 30 EHRR 121; *SC v UK* (2005) 40 EHRR 10
[3] See Residual Special Court for Sierra Leone Statute, article 7; Statute of the Special Court for Sierra Leone, article 7.
[4] See *Prosecutor v Sesay, Kallon and Gbao*
[5] The present author has personal knowledge in relation to this since he represented Mr Rwamakuba.

THE FOUNDATION FOR THE PROTECTION OF VULNERABLE DEFENDANTS

The main legal foundation for the protection of vulnerable defendants is the right to a fair trial.[6] If a defendant suffers from any disability it may affect his or her ability to follow the legal proceedings, prepare his or her defence and answer questions under examination and cross-examination. In this way an inequality of arms or other form of unfairness in the proceedings may arise.

NATIONAL PRACTICE

A variety of measures are taken in national proceedings with respect to vulnerable defendants. In the UK these include determination that a defendant is not fit to plead, the adoption of special measures and the use of intermediaries.

Special measures may include taking the evidence slowly and introducing frequent breaks.

Intermediaries assist the defendant in following the proceedings and alert the court to difficulties of understanding which the defendant may have when the court itself may not appreciate this and assume that the defendant is being evasive.

EARLY INTERNATIONAL PRACTICE: *NUREMBERG*

Gustav Krupp

Gustav Krupp was head of the chief armaments firm, Friedrik Krupp AG, in Germany and Europe during the Second World War. Even during the first world war this company was the major player in German arms being the producer of the Big Berther, named after Krupp's wife, and the U-boats. After World War I, the company secretly contributed to the rearmament of Germany.[7]

Krupp had been a member of the Reich Economic Council and President of the Reich Association of German Industry (Chamber of Commerce) and spearheaded the exclusion of its Jewish members. He opposed the National Socialists and even warned Hindenburg against choosing Hitler

---

[6] Protected in terms of article 6 of the European Convention on Human Rights and Fundamental Freedoms of 1950, the International Covenant on Civil and Political Rights,, article 14 of the International Covenant on Civil and Political Rights of 1966.
[7] See Eugene Davidson, *The Trial of the Germans: An account of the twenty-two defendants before the International Military Tribunal at Nuremberg*, 1966, 26-27.

the day before his appointment as Chancellor. He became a loyal supporter of Hitler after this initial opposition, even being described as a 'super Nazi' by one renowned national socialist.[8] He helped finance the election of 1933 consolidating Hiter's power. In preparing for the punishment of those responsible for the war and its atrocities, the Allied Powers considered this man as one of the most important war criminals.

From 1939, Krupp's health started failing. He suffered a stroke in 1941, leaving him partially paralyzed. At the time of the Nuremberg preparations Krupp was seventy-eight years of age and in hospital with senility. The Tribunal appointed a medical panel, which reported that he could not stand trial. American prosecutor Mr Justice Robert Jackson vigorously argued for a trial in absentia, failing which the replacement of Gustav Krupp's position in the trial with that of his son Alfred Krupp.

The motion to replace father with son was unsuccessful. The Tribunal decided that the indictment would remain pending, in case of recovery of Gustav which never occurred. His son was later tried by a US court which sentenced him to 12 years imprisonment for various crimes including forced labour.

Rudolf Hess

Unlike Gustav Krupp, Rudolf Hess was held fit to stand trial, but this question was in the balance throughout his trial at Nuremberg. As the deputy *führer* to Hitler and the only person in a position to be held responsible for conspiracy to wage war, he was an individual of great significance to the process. Hitler and Göring's claims that he was insane seemed incongruent with the notion of his high status within the regime. He was ultimately sentenced to life imprisonment for his role in the waging of an aggressive war.

Hess missed the major parts of the implementation of the holocaust, because in 1941, he shocked the world including, apparently Hitler, when he flew on an unauthorized peace mission to Scotland.[9] He was detained for the rest of the War.

Hess was present throughout his trial but plainly, at least potentially, fell within the definition of a vulnerable defendant based on all the psychiatric and circumstantial evidence.

The panel of psychiatrists established by the tribunal seemed in agreement that he was suffering from amnesia.[10] Although he made the

---

[8] Fritz Thysson
[9] See Gerhard Weinberg, *A World at Arms, A global History of World War II*, 2nd ed, 2005, at 237-8 [CRAWLEY PUBLIC LIBRARY]
[10] See Eugene Davidson, *The Trial of the Germans: An account of the twenty-two defendants*

extraordinary revelation that he had been faking it half way through the trial there continued to be evidence of mental illness as he read books throughout the trial, refused to cooperate with his lawyer and made what can only be described as a bizarre closing statement.

CONTEMPORARY INTERNATIONAL PRACTICE: MILOSEVIC

One of the cases which perhaps highlights the difficulties of vulnerable defendants in international legal proceedings in the most poignant way is that of Milosevic. As a former president of Serbia, he was perceived as among those most responsible for the atrocities committed in the former Yugoslavia. This notwithstanding his trial was marked with significant health difficulties throughout the trial, ultimately culminating in his death before the conclusion of the trial.[11] What made things even more complicated was the fact that he insisted on self-representation.

On his arrival at The Hague in 2001 he suffered from hypertension and heart problems. He died on the 11 March 2006 among media speculation that he may have been poisoned to silence him or avoid embarrassment of an acquittal, or that he had committed suicide.

In this case a form of special measures were adopted. He was accorded four days of rest every two weeks and subsequently the schedule was reduced to three sessions a week.[12]

On Milosevic's death an investigation was conducted. An investigation of the death was conducted by the Dutch authorities, including an ortopsy. Murder or suicide was excluded and the cause of death was found to be a heart attack.[13]

AREAS OF VULNERABILITY BEFORE THE ICC

The kind of factors which might lead to vulnerability in the case of leaders being tried before international courts may differ from the national experience. The particular domain of the young defendant is removed from the international arena because such offenders will not be tried in international courts. Issues of mental disability involving lack of understanding and low IQ are also likely to be rare.

Other psychiatric problems and health issues on the other hand abound amongst the international defendants. Persons who have been involved in

---

before the International Military Tribunal at Nuremberg, 1966.
[11] See Timothy William Water, ed., *The Milosevic Trial, An Autopsy*, at 70-71.
[12] Ibid., at 70
[13] Ibid., at 72

armed conflict and have become leaders have often seen and experienced atrocities, sometimes from a very young age and sometimes involving their own family members. This is certainly the case with respect to conflicts in countries like Rwanda, Sierra Leone and Sudan, where conflict and death have been endemic within the societies for considerable periods of time. This can lead to significant trauma and or psychiatric conditions.

Some of those involved in armed conflict have come from conditions of abject poverty, been experiencing and fighting war as children and have largely been separated from civilization living in the forest. One such case may be that of *Dominic Ogwen*, a Lord's Resistance Army commander involved in the conflict in Northern Uganda. He has not yet even had his confirmation hearing that was envisaged for the month of August of this year (2015) but has now been put back (at the time of writing).[14] However, it is known that he only speaks his indigenous language of *Acholi* and surrendered straight after coming out of the forest. Given the length and nature of this conflict, it is unlikely that he has had much contact with modern civilization, even within the context of Uganda's cities of Kampala and Entebbe. To what extent he will be in a position to fully appreciate the nature of the charges, let alone the process which he faces is as yet unclear.

ICC PROVISIONS FOR DEALING WITH VULNERABLE DEFENDANTS

The legal framework for the International Criminal Court (hereinafter ICC) draws inspiration from the legal traditions around the world. It is therefore understandable that legal principles are largely codified. While the ICC Statute, Rules of Procedure and Evidence, Regulations of the Court and Regulations of the Registry go into an unprecedented amount of detail for founding documents of international tribunals, there is no section specifically dedicated to the problem of vulnerable defendants from a general perspective. This is despite the fact that, in contrast, detailed provisions have been included on the protection of victims and witnesses.

Regulation 103 of the Regulations of the Court tackles the difficulty of maintaining the health of international defendants in detention during lengthy trials. In terms of this provision, the Registrar is called upon to make arrangements to protect the health and safety of detained persons, and to take measures for detained persons with disabilities. A medical person qualified in psychiatry must be on call at the detention centre and special arrangements must be made for those who are mentally ill and suffer from serious psychiatric conditions.

---

[14] See ICC website: *www.icc-cpi.org*

The problems of vulnerability of defendants in the trial process is however, not expressly provided for. The judges are therefore left to provide for such mechanisms as are necessary to ensure the fairness of the trial. Art 67 of the Rome Statute provides for the right to a fair hearing. This includes, inter alia, the principle that the accused must be informed of the nature, cause and content of the charge in a language which he understands; that he is entitled to adequate time and facilities for preparation of his defence; that he is entitled to legal assistance of his choice; that he should be able to examine witnesses against him and witnesses on his behalf under the same conditions; that he should have the assistance of an interpreter; and that he should not be compelled to testify.

Where there are issues over the mental or physical health of the defendant, then particular care may need to be taken to ensure that there is an understanding of the charges and that there is enough time and appropriate facilities for the preparation of the defence. According to the European Court of Human Rights in *SC v United Kingdom*[15], at par 28, the accused has the right to effective participation in his trial and this includes: 'not only the right to be present, but also to hear and follow the proceedings.' The court adds:

> "effective participation" in this context presupposes that the accused has a *broad understanding of the nature of the trial process* and of *what is at stake* for him or her, including the *significance of any penalty* which may be imposed. It means that he or she, if necessary with the assistance of, for example, an interpreter, lawyer, social worker or friend, should be able to *understand the general thrust of what is said in court*. The defendant should be *able to follow what is said by the prosecution witnesses* and, if represented, to *explain to his own lawyers his version of events, point out any statements with which he disagrees and make them aware of any facts which should be put forward in his defence.* [my emphasis]

It is important to ensure that counsel is appointed who has sufficient competence to manage the case and identify the difficulties of his client and where necessary draw them to the attention of the court and or seek the appointment of a psychiatrist.

In national criminal proceedings, the issue may arise whether the accused is fit to plead, in other words whether he has the mental capacity to understand and address the charges against him. In the United Kingdom. Where the accused is found not to be fit to plead, there will be no conviction. In the event of a finding of responsibility a hospital order will

---

[15] *SC v UK* (2004) 40 EHRR 10.

be made. Where fitness to plead is raised the opinion of two independent psychiatrists is required.

In the international arena the issue may also arise. In the International Criminal Court a procedure is envisaged for this in Rule 135. This stipulates that the Trial Chamber, when discharging its obligations under article 64, paragraph 8 (a) (taking a plea), or for any other reasons, or at the request of a party, order a medical, psychiatric or psychological examination of the accused The Chamber may appoint one or more experts. If the Trial Chamber is satisfied that the accused is unfit to stand trial, then it must order that the trial be adjourned. The trial can be revived in the event that the Trial Chamber is satisfied that the accused has become fit to stand trial.

With respect to witnesses, the main difficulty is going to come with the accused's own testimony. In order to preserve equality of arms, it is necessary to ensure that the accused is in a position to understand and answer questions. If his vulnerability is not properly identified and taken into account, there is a risk that legal findings against him will be made based on a false perception of evasiveness. It is this aspect which has led to the use of intermediaries in national proceedings, a practice which has not thus far formerly been adopted in international criminal rules for accused.

Rule 88 provides the foundation for special measures for accused while giving testimony, although not specifically directed at this. In so far as an accused gives evidence, he is a witness, and can benefit from the effect of this provision. It states that special measures can be taken to facilitate the giving of evidence of for example a traumatized witness.

The issue of an accused's testimony and the right to silence came to the fore in the case of *Prosecutor v Germain Katanga*.[16] In that case, the accused was charged with leading an attack on a village. When the evidence for this charge did not stand up at the end of the case, instead of entering an acquittal, the judges decided, by majority, during deliberations to modify the charges to include contribution based upon the fact, largely contained in admissions of the accused during testimony, that he was in charge of a village where there was an airstrip and where arms were delivered in preparation for the attack by others. The accused chose not to exercise his right to silence in the face of certain charges. Having made that choice he was then subsequently convicted based upon information which he himself had confirmed to the court. The fairness of this is obviously open to question and was the subject of an appeal which failed. However, it

---

[16] see ICC website: www.icc-cpi.int (situations and cases: situation in the Democratic Republic of Congo) https://www.icc-cpi.int/en_menus/icc/situations%20and%20cases/situations/situation%20icc%200104/related%20cases/icc%200104%200106/Pages/democratic%20republic%20of%20the%20congo.aspx [Accessed 15.04.16].

illustrates the enormous difficulties which could be faced by a vulnerable defendant, both in terms of the decision to testify and the testimony itself.

CONCLUSION

Issues relating to the vulnerability of defendants are in their infancy within the international criminal courts and tribunals. These courts have only been operating since the early 1990s, there having been a long gap after the Nuremberg trials.

At Nuremberg panels of psychiatrists were appointed to assess the accused before that court and it is clear that there were issues of vulnerability highlighted by the cases of Krupp and Hess as well as the suicides of Robert Ley and Hermann Goering. It has not been a regular practice to appoint psychiatrists in the recent international criminal trials. Issues of vulnerability have been largely left to the judges to address in a reactive manner, and often from a judicial perspective without proper medical expertise being brought into the fold. At all stages of the proceedings.

When the Rome Statute was negotiated practically every scenario was foreseen and discussed. The issue of the vulnerability of victims and witnesses was addressed extensively. It does not appear that the question of the vulnerability of defendants was given any real consideration as reflected in the texts. This is perhaps partly due to the fact that much of the emphasis was on ensuring that there was no impunity from international crimes, whatever the position or rank of a defendant. The principle of complementarity meant that only those most responsible were likely to be tried before the ICC. These individuals, often convicted in the media long before their trials, could not be seen as in any way vulnerable, especially in the light of the horrible nature of the crimes with which they were being accused.

However, there is obviously a side to this that is not seen or is overlooked by those concerned with international justice. There are no specific mechanisms for addressing the problem. Given the difficulties which may exist in identifying the vulnerable, the vulnerability of defendants before international criminal courts is unlikely to be adequately addressed in the absence of provisions designed to focus on this problem. As things stand it is for judges to address these issues on an ad hoc basis. The experience of the death of Milosevic was a wake up call for the International Criminal Tribunal for the former Yugoslavia. The ICC has made particular provision for ensuring the health of defendants while in detention. However, the lack of other provisions suggests that this is an area that deserves further research and attention by international legislators.

Vulnerable Witnesses and Parties in all Civil Proceedings – Dignity, Respect and The Advocate's Gateway Toolkit 17[1]

FELICITY GERRY QC[2]

It is a truism of some longevity that every civilised society is measured according to how it treats its weaker and less advantaged members. It is probably correct to say that most members of society do not have to attend a court at any stage of their lifetime, much less give evidence in any form of legal proceedings. Almost seventy years ago, an Italian author described courtrooms as "grey hospitals of human corruption". Further, Lord Bingham has observed:

---

[1] Taken in part from an article by Felicity Gerry QC and Jonathan Wheeler for PI Focus Magazine a refereed conference paper for 3rd IARS International Annual Conference: "A victim-led criminal justice system?" and from Toolkit 17 prepared by The Advocate's Gateway working party. The working party was chaired by Felicity Gerry QC and the members were Jonathan Wheeler, President of the Association of Personal Injury Lawyers (APIL), Stephen Glynn, barrister and executive committee member of APIL, David McClenaghan, solicitor and secretary of APIL's Child Abuse Special Interest Group, Lee Moore, former barrister, campaigner and trainer and Peter Dean, barrister specialising in civil proceedings involving vulnerable people.

[2] Felicity Gerry QC is admitted to the Bar of England and Wales and to the Supreme Court of the Northern Territory of Australia. She has been recognised in Chambers and Partners as "a vastly experienced advocate noted for her experience in serious sexual cases, homicides and frauds". Since 2013, Felicity has also held a research active post at Charles Darwin University where she is Chair of the Research and Research Training Committee and higher degree in research coordinator in the School of Law. She runs the indigenous justice stream of the legal clinic where she is supervising the production of a toolkit for advocacy with indigenous people and she is a member of the Management Committee of The Advocate's Gateway. She is also co-author of The Sexual Offences Handbook.

"Few would choose to set foot in a court at any time in their lives if they could avoid it ...".

Those on whom this burden and challenge fall constitute a relatively small minority of the population. Within this small minority, there is a significant percentage of witnesses who, by virtue of their youth, emotional or physical wellbeing or some other factor are vulnerable.[3]

In 2015 a working party for The Advocate's Gateway produced a toolkit for advocacy with vulnerable people in civil proceedings in England and Wales. This paper gives an overview of the current situation in civil proceedings and the content of the new civil toolkit number 17.

It is now commonly accepted that those working in any justice system have to be sensitive to the needs of vulnerable people as well as the stress and trauma of the litigation process. It follows that this applies in civil proceedings and we must work to ensure that the civil justice system, whilst remaining robust, is not abusive to those who participate in it. Witnesses <u>and</u> parties may be vulnerable. This needs to be recognised and our processes adapted to accommodate them to deliver a fair result. It is vital that vulnerable people in all proceedings are supported to be able to give their best evidence. The focus of this paper is domestic and reference is to the law, practice and procedure in England and Wales but an improvement in processes for vulnerable people in English courts has the potential for international effect as litigation is increasingly transnational.

In representing some litigants, particularly in civil compensation claims, often clients have already undergone a bruising experience in the criminal courts. Asylum seekers, vulnerable employees, those who have suffered illness or injury and many others will come to the civil justice system as damaged individuals with long-standing psychological problems. This is not confined to personal injury law. For some, the process itself will trigger vulnerability. In the civil justice system anecdotal evidence is that there are clients who have taken a lower offer than advised in order to avoid the trauma of a final hearing. Some suggest, findings of incapacity may be being made when all a person really seems to need is assistance to communicate. Whether these views are accurate is not the purpose of this paper. What the working party was able to do was to identify where the relevant guidance already sits and how the civil justice system can be improved for vulnerable people.

---

[3] Quote taken from the Northern Ireland Law Commission Report on Vulnerable Witnesses in Civil Proceedings 2011.

On a practical level, the use of intermediaries and of pre-recorded oral evidence, for example, can enable vulnerable witnesses to participate in a hearing in a manner that best meets their needs by ensuring that the evidence they give is the best evidence achievable. Inconsistencies can be agreed on paper without the need to cross-examine at all and advocates need not put an obvious case theory to a vulnerable witness at all. It should already be obvious. Training in this area, of judges, advocates and representatives is vital. If everyone does their job properly, judges need not intervene at all. The Advocate's Gateway has pioneered the sensitive approach to be taken, particularly in cases involving sexual offending. A well prepared representative can take a complainant's account sensitively and a well prepared advocate can effectively challenge the evidence of a witness and show it to be wrong without the witness having to be bullied or humiliated by the experience. It can all be done with dignity and respect, whether the witness is the alleged victim or the accused.

The approach to such cases needs to be balanced and collaborative. It is not a lawyer bashing exercise. It does not require an intermediary in every case nor is it an opportunity for judges to become autocratic or enter the arena. It really is time to recognise that people with vulnerabilities and disabilities can be assisted to fully participate in the civil process whether the matter settles or goes to trial.

The old fashioned adversarial approach is based on historic rules of competence: Calling evidence from women and children and other vulnerable witnesses was believed to be inherently dangerous.[4] Corroboration was required and judges routinely warned that such testimony was unreliable. The modern approach recognises that, given the right assistance, witnesses can be questioned and cross questioned without unnecessary trauma in a balanced way that allows for a fair hearing for all concerned.

This has been recognised and is being applied in criminal and family cases and the civil courts will have to follow suit. Recognition of vulnerabilities at an early stage is vital to ensure that vulnerable witnesses and parties are identified and enabled to effectively participate, largely by facilitating communication. It follows that attention should also be paid to the potential for triggers to vulnerability throughout proceedings. As set out above, civil litigation can cover a wide range of civil and commercial disputes, immigration, employment, housing and public law and so on. The resulting toolkit may also be a useful guide for formal Inquiries such as the *Goddard* Inquiry into institutional responses to child sexual abuse. Toolkit 17 is only a general guide for dealing with vulnerability at all

---

[4] *R v Brasier* (1779) 1 Leach 199; 169 ER 202.

stages of case preparation including where a case is settled, as well as at court. On a typical timeline, a civil case can take up to two years to resolve so there is time to prepare properly. Fortunately, the toolkit production coincided with comprehensive Law Society guidance on meeting the needs of vulnerable clients to which the toolkit refers and which is also an openly available resource[5].

Despite the best efforts of The Association of Personal Injury Lawyers(APIL), the working party found that there is no data on the number of vulnerable people in civil litigation. There is some data on vulnerable court users but it is not complete. By way of examples, the following figures were obtained:

a. Over the last 5 years to the end of 2014, 75,000 cases were heard by the Court of Protection
b. In the year to February 2015, 139,149 accounts were set up by the Court Funds office for children who had received compensation. This does not include those cases where damages are accepted on behalf of a child without court approval by giving a parental indemnity. In addition 7,404 accounts were for Court of Protection awards for vulnerable adults and 1,139 were for protected beneficiaries.
c. The Court Users survey of a small sample of court users in 2009-2010 has very low figures for adult court users who identify themselves as having a long-term illness, health problem or disability. This is not a useful guide as the sample was small (8,782 people), research tends to show self-reporting is unreliable, and the categories do not focus on vulnerability. Advocates should be aware (for example) of the content of the Radford Study[6] into child abuse and neglect in the UK in order to understand that witnesses in any form of civil litigation may present as non-vulnerable but may have a significant background and history as a child.

Even on this limited information, civil cases are dealing with an awful lot of vulnerable people and data and research in the field is clearly inadequate.

The current civil procedure rules[7] provide a wide but unfocussed discretion allowing for the use of technology and adapted court procedures but unfortunately, this is not covered in the directions questionnaire. Updating the questionnaire would be a simple, inexpensive piece of

---

[5] *Meeting the Needs of Vulnerable Clients,* Law Society Publication, http://www.lawsociety.org.uk/Support-services/Advice/Practice-notes/meeting-the-needs-of-vulnerable-clients-july-2015/

[6] NSPPC Study 2011 by Lorraine Radford, Susana Corral, Christine Bradley, Helen Fisher, Claire Bassett, Nick Howat and Stephan Collishaw, Civil Procedure Rules, <http://www.crin.org/docs/1323_child_abuse_neglect_research_PDF_wdf84181_original.pdf>

[7] https://www.justice.gov.uk/courts/procedure-rules/civil

progress. There are also no formal procedures for settlement meetings despite the need to consider the vulnerability of parties although the Law Society guidance now goes some way to addressing this. The toolkit was therefore provided against a background where there is no focussed practice direction in civil proceedings on the issue of vulnerability, no accepted procedure for advocates, representatives or judges to identify vulnerable people in civil proceedings, no specific special measures and no requirements on judges to manage cases in relation to vulnerable witnesses or parties, including where the case involves litigants in person. In this context, the following are imperative:

    a.   As there is no definition of a 'vulnerable witness' or a 'vulnerable party' in the civil justice system where a significant proportion of parties and witnesses are likely to be vulnerable, it is vital for advocates, representatives and judges to seek to identify those who are vulnerable and the assistance they will need to give their best evidence. General risk factors which suggest a witness is vulnerable are outlined in Toolkit 10; 'Identifying Vulnerability in Witnesses and Defendants'[8]

    b.   Vulnerability should be identified at the earliest possible stage and information sharing is key to achieving this. There is currently no bank of available intermediaries, independent sexual violence advisers [IVSA's] or technological facilities to assist in dealing with vulnerable clients or witnesses so the burden is on the advocates, representatives and judges up to the point of settlement or judgment to ensure that efforts are made at every stage to ensure the effective participation of vulnerable parties and witnesses. The need for a Ground Rules hearing should be considered if a vulnerable witness or party is due to give evidence. GRH's are well researched and detailed in toolkit 1 and the GRH checklist.[9] Civil judges should consider 'additional measures' and other reasonable adjustments throughout proceedings. The current rules are passive in that they merely set out a wide discretion.

    c.   Advocates, representatives and judges should be proactive in ensuring that suitable measures are available to enable parties or witnesses to give their best evidence during case preparation, and to be able to effectively participate in settlement procedures, at any hearing and where appropriate, immediately after any hearing

---

[8] The Advocate's Gateway Toolkit 10 <http://www.theadvocatesgateway.org/images/toolkits/10identifyingvulnerabilityinwitnessesanddefendants100714.pdf.>

[9] The Advocate's Gateway Toolkit 1 <http://www.theadvocatesgateway.org/images/toolkits/1groundruleshearingsandthefairtreatmentofvulnerablepeopleincourt060315.pdf and The Advocate's Gateway Ground Rules Hearing checklist < http://www.theadvocatesgateway.org/images/toolkits/groundruleshearingchecklist06032015.pdf >

and/or settlement procedure to ensure effective participation and clear understanding of a result. For example, communication aids are now available such as dolls to indicate positioning of people in allegations of sexual abuse and a 'pause' button for when a witness needs a break.
d. Special consideration should be given to managing and funding cases with interpreters, intermediaries or IVSA's. The latter are a small network of independent advisers. They have been established across England and Wales as part of a government initiative to provide targeted professional support to victims of serious, sexual violent crime.[10]

There is clearly a need for more informed support for vulnerable witnesses and parties in the civil justice system, particularly adults who are at risk of being triggered to self-harm. There is also a need for the provision of training for advocates, representatives and judges, particularly as civil practitioners spend comparatively less time in contested hearings. Those who regularly appear in traumatic cases need to keep their training up to date and be vigilant to the potential for their own secondary stress.

CURRENT RULES AND GUIDANCE

There are no civil procedure rules which deal expressly with vulnerable witnesses or parties. The rules (Part 21 CPR 1998) make specific provision only for children (under 18) and protected parties, those lacking the capacity to conduct litigation within the meaning of Mental Capacity Act 2005. As with fitness to plead procedures in criminal courts, enabling a vulnerable party to participate may avoid the need to find them incapable. At the very least an assessment of measures available should be considered by the court when considering capacity as is is a draconian outcome if someone is prevented from conducting their own litigation when they may only need the assistance of an intermediary or communication aids.

The Civil Procedure Rules (CPR) are clearly designed to have flexibility for the challenges created by the vulnerability of a party (falling short of protected party status) and witnesses. However, there are no specific provisions in this regard. The court is empowered generally under Part 1 and Part 3.1 of the CPR to manage cases in accordance with the overriding objective to achieve justice and this unfettered discretion allows the court to make such orders as it sees fit to further this objective. It might be argued that this allows for flexibility but the risk is that passive rules rely on the

---

[10] *CPS guidance on violence against women* http://www.cps.gov.uk/legal/v_to_z/violence_against_women/index.html#victim

witness or party requesting assistance rather than the system working proactively to facilitate effective participation.

Video link is a valuable resource. Part 34.8 permits the evidence of a witness to be taken by way of a deposition. Hitherto this has been used in proceedings with a foreign element or in cases concerning the terminal illness of a party or witness who may not be alive (or be able) to give evidence at the time of trial (this is a common practice in terminally ill asbestos disease victims for example). The procedure is that the witness' evidence is taken at a time and a place agreed before an examiner of the court who represents the judge.

Unless otherwise directed the examination of the witness must be conducted in the same way as if the witness were giving evidence at the trial (Part 34.9).

The taking of a deposition, requires the deponent to be examined under oath before a judge or examiner of the court (or such other person as may be appointed). This can be a cumbersome procedure and, if being dealt with across jursdictions may mean that the guidance in this toolkit is not familiar to the examiner. As an alternative to obtaining a deposition, evidence by video link will generally be preferable[11] in some cases and has the further advantage that the trial judge will hear the evidence first hand. The recorded evidence is then deployed at trial. For questioning by live link, see also Toolkit 9 Planning to Question Someone Using a Remote Link.[12]

The CPR permit the giving of evidence by video link (part 32.3) but this (and the use of evidence by way of deposition above) is at present against the general rule that factual evidence is to be proved by witnesses giving oral evidence at the trial (part 32.2). Evidence given by way of video link has the advantage over evidence given by way of deposition in that the trial judge will be hearing and seeing the witness first hand and be able to ask questions himself. However the extent to which the court will allow applications of this sort based on the vulnerability of the witness is not easy to predict and in the current climate the application would have to be supported by compelling evidence that the vulnerability is such that it is right to make such an order, certainly in cases concerning claims for damages arising out of historic sexual abuse.

There are currently no rules for case preparation, meetings with experts or settlement meetings and the directions questionnaire does not proactively raise issues of vulnerability. It follows that there are substantial benefits of a revised approach to the collection and presentation of evidence from

---

[11] See *White Book* Vol 1 34.8.6.
[12] The Advocate's Gateway Toolkit 9, <http://www.theadvocatesgateway.org/images/tool kits/9planningtoquestionsomeoneusingaremotelink100714.pdf>

vulnerable parties and witnesses in the civil justice system. Improving the treatment of vulnerable people in the civil justice system brings a greater likelihood of a fair and just hearing and outcome for all the parties in each case. In particular, a revised approach will optimise conditions in which the best evidence can be given, as well as the more effective and efficient use of court time. The Law Society has guidance on meeting the needs of vulnerable clients[13] includes clients with a range of physical and mental health problems, including learning disabilities. There is also a helpful focus for practitioners on the best approach to take when working with clients who lack mental capacity. The guidance is supplemented by an Easy Read guide for clients, supporting them to access solicitors more easily.

It is also important to note that criminal and civil cases can overlap and by November 2015, EU member states will need to have demonstrated that they have modified their domestic laws to give effect to the Victim Directive 2012/29/EU which establishes minimum standards on the rights, support and protection of victims of crime by adopting various means, combining legislative, administrative and practical measures, and taking into account good practices in the field of assistance and protection for victims. To begin to understand how this might interest civil representatives and advocates, it is worth noting that, for the purpose of the directive, a victim is defined as follows:

- a natural person who has suffered harm (including physical, mental or emotional harm or economic loss) directly caused by a criminal offence — regardless of whether an offender is identified, apprehended, prosecuted or convicted and regardless of the familial relationship between them (see Recital 19).
- family members of the deceased victim, who have suffered harm because of person's the death directly caused by a criminal offence (paragraph 1(a)(ii)). The criterion 'harm' should be interpreted in the context of the individual emotional relationship and/or direct material inter-dependence between the deceased victim and the relative(s) concerned.

For witness protection and engagement, there is precedent for the anonymisation of proceedings in relation to vulnerable witnesses and parties. Advocates, representatives and judges should be aware of JXMX (by her mother and litigation friend AXMX) v Dartford and Gravesham NHS Trust [2015] EWCA Civ 96 which considered CPR Rule 39.2(4) which now provides that:

---

[13] Law Society Guide <http://www.lawsociety.org.uk/support-services/advice/practice-notes/meeting-the-needs-of-vulnerable-clients-july-2015>/

The court may order that the identity of any party or witness must not be disclosed if it considers non-disclosure necessary in order to protect the interests of that party or witness.

Some cases will automatically trigger issues of vulnerability because of the topic. It is important to note issues such as human trafficking and forced labour may arise in the civil context so advocates need to be aware of various relevant legalisation including, but not limited to, The Modern Slavery Act 2015, and *Directive 2011/36*/EU of the European Parliament and of the Council of 5 April 2011 on preventing and combating trafficking in human beings. Other areas traditionally seen as "criminal" are increasingly being considered by the civil courts including forced labour, forced marriage and female genital mutilation. These are areas where advocates, representatives and judges should ensure they have specialist knowledge and training on vulnerability in justice systems to include cultural awareness and unconscious bias training.

OTHER JURISDICTIONS

Comparative guidance is available in both criminal and family proceedings. Advocates, representatives and judges should be familiar with the material openly available on The Advocate's Gateway website www.theadvocatesgateway.com, particularly the good practice examples for facilitating communication and enabling vulnerable witnesses and parties to give their best evidence. Toolkit 17 is an overview for use in many different types of civil proceedings, those good practice examples were not repeated but clearly it is examples of good and bad practice which will most assist practitioners. In the context of trauma, Toolkit 17 was produced at the same time as Toolkit 18 on working with traumatised witnesses, defendants and parties. Members of the working party for the civil toolkit also had input into the trauma toolkit. It is hoped that these will both have significant impact in the improvement of the approach to vulnerability in justice systems generally. Ultimately cases in all jurisdictions needed to be conducted with dignity and respect.

One major issue is the lack of definition of vulnerability in civil proceedings. The working party for Toolkit 17 decided not to formulate a definition but to direct those who access the resource to the following definitions in criminal law which are of assistance:

Vulnerable witnesses are defined by section 16 Youth Justice and Criminal Evidence Act 1999 (YJCEA) as:

e.   All child witnesses (under 18); and

f. Any witness whose quality of evidence is likely to be diminished because they:
   i. are suffering from a mental disorder (as defined by the Mental Health Act 1983);
   ii. have a significant impairment of intelligence and social functioning; or
   iii. have a physical disability or are suffering from a physical disorder.

Intimidated witnesses are defined by section 17 YJCEA as those suffering from fear or distress in relation to testifying in the case. Complainants in sexual offences are defined by section 17(4) as automatically falling into this category unless they wish to opt out.

CODES OF CONDUCT - REPRESENTATIVES

Given the court rules are passive and there is no civil practice direction on vulnerability, the Toolkit 17 working party took the view that it was important to set out any obligations on those working in the system. Judges, of course, should be controlling their own court rooms but for advocates and representatives, the system relies on ethical integrity and some regulation. This should ensure that principles of dignity and respect function in court and during out of court preparation. Mandatory principles underpinning the regulatory framework and which may impact on a solicitor's or other regulated representative's interaction with vulnerable people include:
- ensuring that the rule of law is upheld and that justice is properly administered;
- acting with integrity;
- acting in the best interests of each client;
- providing a proper standard of service to each client; and
- behaving in a way that maintains the trust that the public places in representatives.

The new Solicitors Regulatory Authority (SRA) Handbook was published during the course of the preparation of the civil toolkit, on the 30th April 2015[14]. Chapter 1 deals with client care. This chapter is about providing a proper standard of service, which takes into account the individual needs and circumstances of each client. Outcomes centre around the need to treat clients fairly and to ensure that the service provided to *clients* is competent, delivered in a timely manner and takes account of the individual *client's* needs and circumstances. Chapter 2 is about encouraging

---

[14] See also for example the code of conduct for members of the Chartered Institute of Legal Executives: http://www.cilex.org.uk/membership/code_of_conduct.aspx

equality of opportunity and respect for diversity, and preventing unlawful discrimination. The requirements apply in relation to age, disability, gender reassignment, marriage and civil partnership, pregnancy and maternity, race, religion or belief, sex and sexual orientation. There are also duties in relation to evidence and not taking unfair advantage. Overall, solicitors and other representatives must act in a manner which promotes the proper operation of the justice system. As set out above under case preparation, the Law Society has issued comprehensive guidance to help solicitors meet the needs of vulnerable clients. The guidance sets out good practice examples including how to:

- identify vulnerable clients;
- identify their needs at an early stage and respond appropriately;
- communicate with them more effectively;
- address issues they may have relating to mental capacity;
- work with third parties who can assist them and you to achieve the best possible legal outcomes.

CODES OF CONDUCT - ADVOCATES

The Bar Standards Board Handbook 2014 provides the code of conduct for barristers who should ensure that the interests of vulnerable clients and their needs are taken into account [oC14], and should do what they reasonably can to ensure that the client understands the process and what to expect from it and from their barrister. It also states that barristers should also try to avoid any unnecessary distress to the client [gC41].

g. However, the Core Duties with which barristers are required to comply, include the duty –
- To observe your duty to the court in the administration of justice [CD1].
- To act in the best interests of each client [CD2].
- To act with honesty and integrity [CD3].
- Not to behave in a way which is likely to diminish the trust and confidence which the public places in you or in the profession [CD5].
- Not to discriminate unlawfully against any person [CD8].

h. Representatives are subject to similar duties, to uphold the rules of law and proper administration of justice, and to provide a proper standard of service to clients including vulnerable clients [Principles 1 and 5, Representatives Regulation Authority Code of Conduct].

These duties mean that all members of the Bar have some responsibility to assist the court to identify and appropriately respond to the vulnerability of parties and other witnesses. In addition, it is suggested advocates should, as part of their duty to assist the court in the administration of justice, assist the court as a public authority in its duty to act compatibly with the European Convention on Human Rights, especially articles 6 and 8. Although the Bar Council has encouraged the creation of a required training programme in this area[15], no compulsory course yet exists.

Representatives, advocates and judges should be aware that they too are potentially vulnerable to the adverse and unavoidable impact of secondary traumatic stress. They need to be alert to the symptoms and have steps in place enabling them to manage and metabolize any traumatic material to which they may be exposed during the legal process. Any reactivity could potentially re-traumatise vulnerable witnesses or parties, impeding their efficacy and communication in court[16]. This is dealt with in more detail in Toolkit 18 which deals with trauma which demonstrates the importance of accessing, understanding and using all the toolkits on The Advocate's Gateway website.

IDENTIFYING VULNERABILITY OF PARTIES AND WITNESSES

Advocates should try to establish at the earliest possible stage whether a client could be considered 'vulnerable'. Ideally this will be at the first meeting or conference with a client. Some types of vulnerability will be more obvious than others. The Advocates' Gateway Toolkit 10 *Identifying Vulnerability In Witnesses and Defendants*[17] contains some good practice example questions to the client which may assist the advocate in ascertaining vulnerability and / or where the person is taking medication. However, self-reporting is not the only or even the most reliable way of ascertaining vulnerability. Certain behaviour, characteristics or circumstances may also suggest vulnerability. Toolkit 10 also provides a helpful list of behavioural characteristics or circumstances that may warrant further consideration.

---

[15] In a press release dated 1 July 2013 (responding to the Advocacy Training Council's report *Raising the Bar – the Handling of Vulnerable Victims, Witnesses and Defendants in court*).
[16] Secondary Trauma and Burnout in Attorneys: Effects of Work with Clients who are Victims of Domestic Violence and Abuse <http://www.americanbar.org/content/newsletter/publications/cdv_enewsletter_home/expertLevin.html > and 24 Pace Law. Review. 245 (2003-2004) Vicarious Trauma in Attorneys; Levin, Andrew P.; Greisberg, Scott and Secondary Traumatic Stress in Attorneys and their Administrative Support Staff Working with Trauma Exposed Clients <www.ncbi.nlm.nih.gov/pubmed/22134453>

[17] Ibid n8

It is important to remember that vulnerability may not be constant, consistent or continuous within an individual. Someone who would be regarded as vulnerable at the initial stage of a case might not be at the final hearing and vice versa. Vulnerability may be transient or situational. Advocates, representatives and judges should therefore consider the issue of vulnerability at the time of the relevant meeting or hearing.

It follows that the issue of vulnerability should be kept under review. Individual personal factors (for example, age, incapacity, impairment or medical condition), environmental factors, or a combination of the two can give rise to vulnerability. For example, an environmental factor, such as being in the courtroom or seeing one of the parties might 'trigger' anxiety. It may also be necessary to obtain and share information with other professionals and organisations working with the client, such as the police, social workers, medical or mental health professionals or other support workers.

An expert may be necessary to help ascertain the level and extent of vulnerability, so consideration should be given at the earliest stage as to whether an application under Part 35CPR should be made to the court. The type of expert required (if any) will depend heavily on the circumstances of the case. It should be remembered however that expert evidence is to be restricted to that which is reasonably required to resolve the proceedings: CPR 35.1. In addition, information may be helpful from treating doctors and professionals. Representatives, advocates and judges should bear in mind that vulnerability can be transient or fluctuating, and is not the same as capacity. The issue of vulnerability should therefore be regularly and proactively reviewed. Vulnerability may only become apparent or heightened in certain circumstances. For example, a client's vulnerability may not be apparent when in a meeting/conference, but may become apparent or heightened when at court, during evidence or in meetings with professionals.

Representatives, advocates and judges should be familiar with *Achieving Best Evidence in Criminal Proceedings: Guidance on Interviewing Victims and Witnesses, and Guidance on Using Special Measures* (March 2011) (the ABE guidance)[18]. It relates solely to criminal proceedings but is a detailed analysis of good practice that has developed for the interviewing of children and vulnerable witnesses and the principles should be readily applicable to civil law cases. For those involved in cross jurisdictional cases

---

[18] Achieving Best Evidence in Criminal Proceedings: Guidance on Interviewing Victims and Witnesses and Using Special Measures, (UK: 2011 <http://www.cps.gov.uk/publications/docs/best_evidence_in_criminal_proceedings.pdf > See also: Raising the Bar: The Handling of Vulnerable Witnesses, Victims and Defendants in Court (UK 2011) http://www.advocacytrainingcouncil.org/images/word/raisingthebar.pdf

there is also Commonwealth guidance: See in particular the Bench Book for Children Giving Evidence In Australian Courts[19] and the 'interviewing children' section of the Australian Institute of Family Studies library.

It may become apparent to the representative or advocate that an unrepresented party, or a witness who is not a party, may be vulnerable. Part of the advocate's duty is to raise this with the judge at the earliest stage, to consider whether to obtain expert evidence (and how to fund it if the vulnerable witness is not a party) and (in the case of a witness) to consider whether the court should be invited to join that person as an intervener or even a party. If the issue only arises at a late stage, for example during that witness's or party's evidence, it is likely to be necessary to propose an adjournment to allow for assessment of the need for additional measures. Once it is apparent that additional measures or adjustments are needed, particularly during contested hearings, there will almost certainly need to be a Ground Rules type hearing (guidance about which is provided below).

RESOURCES

In order to make use of the civil toolkit effective, it was our working party view that representatives, advocates and judges should be aware of the following studies so that, in the absence of training they can be properly prepared to facilitate the best evidence from vulnerable witnesses and parties:

   a. The MIND 2013 report 'At Risk Yet Dismissed'. The study focuses on experiences of people with mental health problems in the criminal justice system. It reports that 1 in 4 people in England and Wales are estimated to have a mental health problem. Participants found the court process intimidating. Some dropped their cases, others were so severely affected that they went into crisis, self-harming and attempting suicide. Cross-examination by the defence was found to be very distressing, especially the experiences of being mocked and accused of lying. Good practice and enabling examples included pre-court visits, preparation and information, special measures, the judge intervening on their behalf.[20]
   b. The MIND report, 'Achieving Justice for Victims and Witnesses with Mental Distress: A mental health toolkit for prosecutors and advocates,' gives excellent, good practice guidance on how to support people to give their best evidence.[21]

---

[19] Bench Book for Children giving evidence in Australian Courts 2012 http://www.aija.org.au/Child%20Witness%20Bch%20Bk/Child%20Witness%20BB%20Update%202012.pdf
[20] MIND Report, http://www.mind.org.uk/media/642011/At-risk-yet-dismissed-report.pdf
[21] MIND toolkit, http://www.mind.org.uk/media/207147/Prosecutors__toolkit.pdf

Vulnerable Witnesses and Parties in all Civil Proceedings

c. The CPS Violence Against Women and Girls Report 2013. The engagement of ISVA's is given as a good practice guidance in cases of sexual violence against women and girls who enter the criminal justice system.[22]
d. The Prison Reform Trust report on access to justice highlights the need for trained intermediaries to work with vulnerable defendants in the criminal justice system. The value of using intermediaries in the civil justice system is axiomatic.[23]
e. The Vulnerable Witnesses & Children Working Group Report Final March 2015 set up by the President of the Family Division emphasizes the need for the training of advocates and members of the judiciary and the need for the funding of intermediaries. It also gives guidance on good practice.[24]
f. The Valuing People Now: The Delivery Plan 2010-2011 (Department of Health)[25]

CHILDREN AND YOUNG PEOPLE

Persons under the age of 18 should be automatically regarded as vulnerable. This accords with well researched concepts reflected in International Law, particularly the Convention on the rights of the Child.[26] A grant of party status to a child or young person leaves the court with a wide discretion to determine the extent of the role which s/he should play in the proceedings. In *Re LC (Children)* [2014] UKSC 1 Lady Hale, while noting an *"increasing recognition of children as people with a part to play in their own lives, rather than as passive recipients of their parents' decisions"*, identified a number of possible options which could be used if necessary to limit the role of the child or young person as a party. For example –

- Adduce a witness statement by the child or young person, or a report by the child or young person's guardian.
- Permit cross-examination of the other parties on the child or young person's behalf.
- Permit submissions to be made on the child or young person's behalf.

---

[22] CPS Report, http://www.cps.gov.uk/publications/docs/cps_vawg_report_2013.pdf
[23] PRISON REFORM TRUST report, http://www.prisonreformtrust.org.uk/portals/0/documents/fairaccesstojustice.pdf
[24] FAMILY DIVISION REPORT, https://www.judiciary.gov.uk/wp-content/uploads/2015/03/vwcwg-report-march-2015.pdf
[25] DEPARTMENT OF HEALTH Deliviry Plan, http://base-uk.org/sites/base-uk.org/files/[user-raw]/11-06/valuing_people_now_delivery_plan_2010-11.pdf
[26] ICCPR, http://www.ohchr.org/en/professionalinterest/pages/crc.aspx

The extent to which the court should permit the child or young person who is a party to be present in court will be in the court's discretion, and will very much depend on the child or young person's age, wishes and feelings, level of understanding, and the issues for determination before the court. Some children may have vulnerabilities other than age. Regard should be had to some of the matters listed in relation to adults below.

ADULT WITNESSES AND PARTIES

There is currently no data available to indicate whether there has been a recent increase in the number of vulnerable adult witnesses in the civil justice system. There is however a rising tide of awareness that certain groups of adults are particularly vulnerable and are accessing the civil justice system both represented and unrepresented. It is important to take into account the views of the individual witness or the party. Vulnerable people are not a homogenous group and not everyone with a disability will automatically be vulnerable or would wish to be regarded as such. Equally, advocates, representatives and judges should note that parties or witnesses who appear to be robust or resistant to assistance may in fact be fearful about the impact of their vulnerabilities on the outcome of their case; for example, concern that disclosure of a mild learning disability or mental health history could negatively impact on the assessment of their claim. They may also be embarrassed or ashamed of their vulnerability and do all they can to hide or mask it.

There are many ways in which adults participating in civil proceedings may require assistance due to vulnerability, not only to assist them but also to ensure that proceedings can run as smoothly and efficiently as possible; the following list is not exhaustive but provides a guide to the most common examples that representatives and advocates may encounter in practice.

Violence and Sexual Abuse

Special consideration should be given to identifying cases where there is a risk of vulnerable witnesses and/or parties self-harming, attempting and/or committing suicide. People who have experienced sexual abuse in childhood are an at-risk group. Representatives, advocates and judges should anticipate that legal proceedings may well be challenged or interrupted when a witness or party is 'triggered' into recalling a traumatic experience. The re-traumatised witness or party may cope in ways that are instinctive to them but confusing to other people. Witnesses or parties may dissociate, minimize, or try to control unrelated aspects of their environment. They may experience terror, uneasiness, flashbacks, body memories, freeze, go blank, become inarticulate and experience feelings they felt at the time of initial trauma. For example, representatives and advocates should try to ensure that any hearings, settlement meetings and/or meetings with experts, do not coincide with the anniversary date of the abusive event.

Sensitive timing and pacing are required when questioning a vulnerable witness or party to ensure the witness does not become overwhelmed, potentially re-traumatised or unable to communicate. Representatives, advocates and judges need to be aware as that sexual abuse, particularly involving a family member, is linked to a sense of stigma and painful shame which when triggered may result in the witness becoming re-traumatised. Representatives, advocates and judges should be as aware as possible of traumatic events in the past history and the likely stress on adult victims of knowing or fearing that they may have to discuss those matters and/or encounter another party or witness in a settlement meeting or at court. This may result in them refusing to engage in proceedings or to comply with court directions about providing evidence. An adult victim's confidence and trust can disappear in an instant.

There is currently no decision preventing a litigant in person cross-examining a vulnerable witness or opposing party despite the obvious effect on the giving of best evidence. Advocates should be aware of the the Convention arguments in *Re C* [2014] EWFC 44 in the Family Division and given that by rule 32.1(3) CPR the court can limit cross-examination and rule 32.3 gives the court the discretion to 'allow a witness to give evidence through a video link or by other means'. Reasonable adjustments can be made to avoid humiliation. In extreme cases, this ought to allow for the witness to answer written questions set out by the litigant in person in advance where the judge and the opposing advocate can then also ensure they are suitable.

Representatives and advocates should be aware of the possible detrimental impact on vulnerable adult survivors of sexual abuse of knowing that highly personal and sensitive information about their past histories could become 'common knowledge' in civil proceedings. In these situations representatives and advocates should consider whether and, if so, how such information can be shared on a need-to-know-only basis. The following sets out some of the major areas of vulnerability and what responses may be necessary:

Past Medical History

Representatives and advocates should be aware of the potential embarrassment for vulnerable adult parties or witnesses of realising that aspects of their past medical histories may need to be disclosed within proceedings. In these situations representatives and advocates should consider whether and if so, how, such information can be shared on a 'need-to-know-only' basis.

Physical Disability

Practitioners and courts should accommodate those persons with physical disabilities making the appropriate adjustments.

Hidden Disability

In relation to hidden disabilities such as specific language impairment, dyslexia, dyspraxia, dyscalculia and attention deficit disorder see Toolkit 5 on planning to question someone with hidden disabilities.[27]

Stammering

Representatives and advocates need to exercise great patience with vulnerable witnesses or parties who stammer. Time must be given to allow them to communicate. Reasonable adjustments such as non-speaking methods should be considered to enable communication by alternative means. Further guidance is given in Toolkit 5 Planning to Question someone with 'hidden' disabilities; specific language impairment, dyslexia and other related specific learning difficulties.[28]

Learning Disability

Representatives and advocates may need to request extra time when proposing the time estimate of a hearing in cases where an adult party or witness has learning difficulties, or they may need to make arrangements for an intermediary, an adult services social worker or an advocate to attend court with the adult to assist them in following and understanding proceedings.

Mental Health

Representatives and advocates should be aware of the possible stressful effects of proceedings on adult parties or witnesses who are vulnerable

---

[27] The Advocate's Gateway Toolkit 5 http://www.theadvocatesgateway.org/images/toolkits/5Hiddendisabilities 211013.pdf
[28] Ibid. n21 and see http://www.stammeringlaw.org.uk/services/courts.htm

due to mental health difficulties and to consider practical ways in which such stress can be reduced. Guidance is given in the MIND Mental Health Toolkit[29]

Deafness

In *Re C (A Child)* [2014] EWCA Civ 128 the Court of Appeal gave guidance about the correct approach to be applied in care proceedings involving profoundly deaf parents. In particular –
- It is necessary for all agencies concerned to understand that communicating with a profoundly deaf person is not simply a matter of interpretation or translation. There will be a need for expert insight and support by a suitably qualified person at the earliest stage. It is the duty of those acting for the parents to identify the disabilities as a factor at the earliest stage.
- The parents and the local authority should make the court aware of the disabilities and need for special measures as a matter of case management.
- An expert should be appointed so that the impact of the disability can be addressed at a case management hearing. In the case of a profoundly deaf person consideration should be given to the use of an intermediary to communicate with the local authority and the court.

Sexuality and gender identity

Representatives and advocates should be aware of the possible stressful effects of participating in proceedings involving adults who are vulnerable due to the impact of issues relating to their sexuality or gender identity.

Ground Rules Hearings

Ground Rules Hearings (GRHs) are a form of case management hearing in criminal cases. GRHs should be required in cases in which an intermediary is appointed and are considered good practice when a witness or defendant has communication needs. GRHs are not yet regularly used in civil proceedings but it is good practice to have a GRH where a witness or party has communication needs or is vulnerable for some other reason, and arguably where there is a litigant in person who is an alleged perpetrator cross-examining an alleged victim. The court and the parties

---

[29] CPS Guidance, http://www.cps.gov.uk/publications/docs/mind_toolkit_for_prosecutors_and_advocates.pdf

should be particularly alive to the types of difficulties that could give rise to communication issues - mental disorder; learning disability and physical disability and the variety of measures and approaches that will be necessary. For further guidance see toolkit 1 ground rules hearings and the fair treatment of vulnerable people in court[30].

Additional Measures and other Adjustments

In civil cases, regard should be had to the possibility of adopting where appropriate the special measures which are available in the criminal courts for vulnerable and intimidated witnesses. They are set out in ss23-30 YJCEA 1999 and include –

- Screening the witness from the accused.
- Giving evidence by live link.
- Giving evidence from a private location.
- Removal of wigs and gowns by advocates and judges[31].
- Evidence being via pre-recorded video interview.
- Giving evidence via an intermediary.
- Giving evidence via an interpreter.
- Using communication aids.

The Crown Prosecution Service (CPS) guidance on vulnerable witnesses also requires prosecutors to consider whether the witness would benefit from more informal arrangements such as pre-trial visits and having regular breaks while giving their evidence[32].

In addition to special measures, the YJCEA also contains the following provisions intended to enable vulnerable or intimidated witnesses to give their best evidence:

- Mandatory protection of the witness from cross-examination by the accused in person: a prohibition on an unrepresented defendant from cross-examining vulnerable child and adult victims in certain classes of cases involving sexual offences.
- Discretionary protection of the witness from cross-examination by the accused in person: in other types of offence, the court has discretion to prohibit an unrepresented defendant from cross-examining the victim in person.
- Restrictions on evidence and questions about a complainant's sexual behaviour: the Act restricts the circumstances in which

---

[30] Ibid n9
[31] Rarely worn in civil proceedings.
[32] CPS Guidance < http://www.cps.gov.uk/victims_witnesses/going_to_court/vulnerable.html>

the defence can bring evidence about the sexual behaviour of a complainant in cases of rape and other sexual offences.
- Reporting restrictions.

Although the discretion in the Civil Procedure Rules is wide, it is suggested that the provisions of the YJCEA can form a useful guide, along with possible appropriate additional measures and other adjustments which may include –

- Provision of separate waiting areas or reserved, secure conference rooms if the witness/party feels intimidated by others involved in the case.
- Making arrangements for the vulnerable witness to arrive at court or leave the court by a different entrance to avoid meeting others in the case.
- Requesting that cases involving vulnerable witnesses or parties are given priority in the list so the witness/party does not suffer unnecessary anxiety or stress due to long waiting times.
- Allowing a representative of an advocacy service (for example, provided by Mencap, POhWER or the Elfrida Society) to be present during meetings, conferences and in court with the party/witness.
- Allowing longer periods for a witness/party to file and serve evidence.
- Judges allowing adequate time after handing down judgment for parties to go though it with their advocates.
- Provision of sign language interpreters and possibly a deaf relay interpreter or Registered Intermediary in cases where the party or witness has a hearing disability. Registered Intermediaries who are themselves deaf can communicate with deaf witnesses in their first language and adapt communication as appropriate. This is preferable to using a deaf relay interpreter whose role is only to translate language. Registered Intermediaries have a wider role in that they can monitor communication, alert the court to any difficulties that arise and adapt communication further to ensure that the deaf witness understands and is understood. Whilst the role of a deaf Registered Intermediary may encompass some delay interpreting the remit is broader and can offer a more comprehensive solution. Registered Intermediaries will also advise the court in relation to suitable sign language interpreters that meet the deaf person's communication needs and monitor the interpreting process to ensure understanding.

- Advocates being required to adjust their style (e.g. fewer leading questions, no 'tagged' questions) or language of questioning (e.g. simple and straightforward language, short sentences).
- Providing the witness/party with a simple way to communicate the need for an extra break (either directly the court or through an intermediary), for example a 'pause' card on the table.
- Providing the witness/party with a way of alleviating stress and maintaining concentration whilst giving evidence, e.g. a stress toy.
- Where the witness is giving evidence by live video link but may become distressed by one or more parties seeing their face, positioning or covering the screen so their face cannot be seen but they can be heard.

Vulnerable witnesses and parties should be consulted about the proposed additional measures. However, representatives, advocates and the court should be alert to the fact that it is not uncommon for witnesses to change their mind about additional measures. There should therefore be some flexibility in arrangements. A careful balance must be reached, however, to ensure that additional measures or other adjustments to ensure the party/witness can give their 'best evidence' do not diminish the value of that evidence or the weight which can be placed on it. Similarly, where the witness/party's evidence forms the basis of allegations made against another party, care must be taken that that party's article 6 rights are not breached.

Assistance to Vulnerable Parties and Witnesses

Although there is no special or additional measures regime in the civil courts in England and Wales, there are sources of expertise and guidance as well as several recent reviews and reports making recommendations about what <u>should</u> happen. Practice is however erratic.
Interpreters

a. There is guidance on interpreters within civil proceedings in England which sets out the court's responsibility to fund interpreters for deaf and hearing impaired litigants (presumably including witnesses) and for foreign language speakers. [33]
b. *Sign language interpreters/BSL interpreters* are qualified professionals who are skilled in the interpretation of English into BSL and vice versa and are accountable to their registration body, the NRCPD. All SLIs working in legal settings must be qualified and registered

---

[33] https://www.justice.gov.uk/courts/interpreter-guidance

Vulnerable Witnesses and Parties in all Civil Proceedings

(RSLI) and should also have experience and/or specific training in working in legal settings. It is important that the deaf person in court understands the interpreters provided; difficulties can arise with interpreters from different areas of the country, in working with deaf children or young people, if the deaf person has idiosyncratic signs or if the interpreter is just not well-matched to the deaf person. A deaf Registered Intermediary (RI), the court interpreter or an independent expert RSLI will advise if this is the case and may recommend a change of interpreter(s) or the use of a different interpreter(s) with particular skills, or the recruitment of a deaf interpreter to the interpreting team.

c. It is worth noting that there are free tools available on the internet that provide instant translations, free of charge, in most languages – see, for example, www.google.com/language_tools, although these will not adequately take the place of an interpreter/intermediary where one is needed.

Key Points when using interpreters

- Use registered, qualified interpreters with legal training and experience. It is not appropriate to use civil members or friends as interpreters as you have no way of monitoring the accuracy of the interpretation and they are not qualified.
- The role of the interpreter is to translate from one language to another. It is not appropriate to ask their opinion or advice.
- Remember to take account of the fact that there will be a time lag whilst the interpretation process takes place.
- Remember that interpreters are obliged to interpret everything that is spoken or signed.
- Remember that English is a second language for those who communicate in another language (including sign language). Do not expect the person to be able to read written documents without assistance. Written documents will also need to be translated.
- Interpreters need to be supplied with documentation to provide them with some background information and contextual understanding so that they can translate accurately in the court.
- Consideration should be given to the importance of written translation rather than oral interpretation. Valuable information is available in the criminal context in Directive 2010/64/EU of the European Parliament and of the Council of 20 October 2010 on the right to interpretation and translation in criminal proceedings.

Intermediaries

Intermediaries provide skilled support to enable communication with vulnerable witnesses within the criminal justice system, and there are precedents for intermediaries to work with vulnerable witnesses and other parties in the civil courts. The role of an intermediary is to improve access for vulnerable people. This can include vulnerable parents who are required to give evidence in civil proceedings. They can assist by providing practical information about the needs of the parents or of the child to the court and can also assist the witness to give evidence by supporting their communication. This may include helping them to prepare to give evidence, to understand court documents and court processes. Intermediaries can assist by –

- Carrying out an initial assessment of the person's communication needs.
- Providing advice to professionals on how a vulnerable person communicates, their level of understanding and how it would be best to question them whilst they are giving evidence.
- Directly assisting in the communication process by helping the vulnerable person to understand questions and helping them to communicate their responses to questions.
- Writing a report about the person's specific communication needs.
- Assisting with court familiarisation.

Sometimes the same witness is involved in both criminal and civil proceedings. In these circumstances the best practice would be for the *same intermediary* to provide communication support in both settings, to ensure continuity for the witness and also to avoid unnecessary cost through duplication of assessment and rapport building. This has happened, but is rare. Whilst the Ministry of Justice (MoJ) operates a scheme of Registered Intermediaries, it is not currently available for civil court witnesses. For more information contact the Witness Intermediary Scheme (WIS) operated by the National Crime Agency socwitnessint@nca.x.gsi.gov.uk In civil cases most intermediaries will be operating outside the WIS and in these circumstances they will be non-registered intermediaries.

The intermediary should be matched according to their communication specialism, their availability and, if possible, their geographic location. Funding must be agreed on a case by case basis as there is no standard procedure in civil courts. Intermediaries are not expert witnesses; they are 'a person who facilitates two way communication between the vulnerable witness and the other participants in the legal process, to ensure that their communication is as complete, accurate and coherent as possible'.[34]

Registered Intermediaries funded by The Ministry of Justice and Independent Sexual Violence Advisers [ISVA's] funded by the Home Office are only available to support vulnerable witnesses in the criminal justice system. No similar facility exists or is currently planned to support vulnerable witnesses in civil proceedings but there are independent organisations who may be approached for funded assistance. See *Intermediaries Step by Step Toolkit 16*.[35]

Interviewers

When the evidence of a vulnerable witness is required for civil proceedings, there are different ways that best evidence can be achieved. Some witnesses have a police interview or joint interview conducted within ABE guidance and therefore available on DVD. Whether or not this interview is used within criminal proceedings, it can be used as evidence in civil proceedings subject to the rules of disclosure.[36] Sometimes an existing police interview is not of sufficient quality, or does not cover some essential issues, in which case an additional filmed interview may be required for civil proceedings. Sometimes witnesses have not been interviewed within ABE guidance (perhaps because of their young age, or because their communication needs have been seen as too complex). In both of the above situations, alternative interview arrangements may be needed. Forensic interviewing of children is a skilled task, and where the child's needs are particularly complex, better evidence may be obtained through specialist interviewers.[37]

Cross-examination

Some vulnerable witnesses are cross-examined live at court by advocates, with or without intermediary support. More radical alternatives are for the questions to be put to the witness by a third party, and/or to pre-record the cross-examination. One advantage of the lack of any formal special or additional measures regime is that the civil courts can innovate. A pilot

---

[34] *R v Secretary of State for Justice and Cheltenham Magistrates' Court and Crown Prosecution Service and Just for Kids Law (intervener)* [2014] EWHC 1944 (Admin) at para 3.
[35] The Advocate's Gateway Toolkit 17 <http://www.theadvocatesgateway.org/images/toolkits/16intermediaries stepbystep060315.pdf>
[36] http://www.cps.gov.uk/publications/docs/third_party_protocol_2013.pdf Disclosure of information in cases of alleged child abuse and linked criminal and care directions hearing (October 2013).
[37] Triangle provides specialist interviewers for children and young people up to the age of 25 (see http://www.triangle.org.uk/what-we-do/intermediaries).

of pre-recorded cross-examination is currently underway in the criminal courts.

Witness/Victim Support

There is no formal witness support system within the civil courts. Witness Service, the national charity supporting victims and witnesses, is clear that its role is with victims and witnesses of crime. It is not clear if this extends to victims of criminal offences giving evidence in civil proceedings

OBTAINING EVIDENCE AND SHARING EVIDENCE

It is essential to think widely and carefully about any professionals or services who may have information about a vulnerable person in order that the Court has before it all relevant information. There are many sources of evidence that might be available in a civil case to provide information about the level and nature of vulnerability in a party or a witness and how to put in place the necessary measures to assist the vulnerable witness. It is therefore important for advocates to understand the most effective ways of obtaining that evidence.

Information being sought for this purpose is likely to be very sensitive and of a personal and private nature. Issues of confidentiality of information are likely to arise when obtaining the information and when considering to whom it should be disclosed. These issues will need to be considered at every stage in a civil case. The Article 6 and Article 8 rights, both of the witness and of those parties involved in the case, are likely to be engaged.

Much will depend on whether the witness is in agreement with the information being sought, or not, on whether the witness is an adult or a child, and whether or not the witness is a party to the civil court proceedings.

Particular sources of information

If a witness or party has already been identified as vulnerable in criminal proceedings, then the first task for the civil court will be to establish if that witness is a potential witness in the civil proceedings. If so, then the civil court will need to establish the following:-

- What information is already available about the witness and any potential vulnerability? What reports/ assessments have already been obtained? What arrangements are being put in place to support that witness?

- What is the timing of the criminal case? Will it be before any civil court hearing involving the same issues? Should the civil case wait for the criminal case? The impact of giving evidence twice needs to be carefully considered.
- If the criminal case has already taken place, or is going to take place before the civil case, consideration should be given to obtaining the transcripts of any evidence given by the relevant witness in the criminal case. If the criminal case is yet to take place, consideration should be given to whether any of the advocates or professionals will attend the criminal proceedings from the civil proceedings. Obtaining the transcripts may avoid, or shorten, the evidence required in a civil case which will be particularly relevant when managing the needs and requirements relating to vulnerable witnesses.
- It is likely that a vulnerable party or witness (adult or child) will have had contact with the medical services and may also be a patient with the Community Mental Health Team (CMHT), Child and Adolescent Mental Health Service (CAMHS), and /or the Community Drug and Alcohol Service (CDAS). Any information from such professionals is likely to be essential to determine the issues of vulnerability in the civil court.

USE OF EXPERTS

It is important to note that all necessary measures should be taken when a vulnerable party is being assessed by an expert to ensure that the expert evidence is produced on a sound evidential basis. On the point of whether a witness or party is vulnerable or not, permission to instruct an expert or an assessor must be sought from the court at the earliest opportunity and no later than the Case Management Hearing. If there is uncertainty about the existence, type or impact of a person's vulnerability, expert advice should be sought. If there is a social worker involved who has sufficient expertise s/he may be able to provide this. Alternatively it may be necessary to obtain an opinion from an expert witness such as a psychologist or psychiatrist or from an intermediary. An intermediary is not an expert witness but can assist by carrying out an assessment of the communication needs and abilities of the witness specifically in relation to communication within legal proceedings and facilitating communication. Parties and the court must be clear about who is to be instructed to report and the purpose of their report.

LITIGANTS IN PERSON (SELF-REPRESENTED LITIGANTS)

Figures for litigants in person are not collated in the civil courts. The Master of the Rolls, Lord Dyson, told a Commons Select Committee in 2011 that the civil courts had experienced a significant impact from a rise in litigants in person[38]. The term 'litigant in person' is the sole term used to describe individuals who exercise their right to conduct legal proceedings on their own behalf. This applies to proceedings in all courts – family, criminal and civil. The term encompasses those preparing a case for trial or hearing, those conducting their own case at a trial or hearing and those wishing to enforce a judgment or to appeal. There are a number of reasons why individuals may choose to represent themselves rather than instruct a lawyer in civil cases –

- Many do not qualify for public funding, either financially or because of the nature of their case. One of the consequences of the Legal Aid, Sentencing and Punishment of Offenders Act 2012 is that public funding in many civil cases (particularly in private law) is rarely available.
- Some cannot afford a solicitor or may distrust lawyers.
- Others believe that they will be better at putting their own case across to the court.

It is important to remember that most litigants in person are stressed and worried, operating in an alien environment in what for them is a foreign language. They are trying to grasp concepts of law and procedure about which they may be totally ignorant. They may well be experiencing feelings of fear, ignorance, frustration, bewilderment and disadvantage, especially if appearing against a represented party. The outcome of the case may have a profound effect and long-term consequences upon their life. They may have agonised over whether the case was worth the risk to their health and finances, and therefore feel passionately about their situation. While many of these circumstances apply generally to litigants in person, they are likely to be particularly relevant in civil proceedings where the issues are usually highly emotive and where the stakes are often extremely high.

Advocates should maintain patience and an even-handed approach in cases involving litigants in person, particularly where the litigant in person is being oppressive or aggressive towards another party or their representative or towards the court or tribunal. In particular, it is important to try and remain understanding, so far as possible, as to what might lie

---

[38] Parliamentary Report <http://www.publications.parliament.uk/pa/cm201415/cmselect/cmjust/311/31109.htm >

behind their behaviour. Maintaining a balance between assisting and understanding what the litigant in person requires, while protecting their represented opponent against the problems that can be caused by the litigant in person's lack of legal and procedural knowledge, is the key issue for the court – and for advocates – in these situations.

The disadvantages faced by litigants in person stem from their lack of knowledge of the law and court or tribunal procedure. For many their perception of the court or tribunal environment will be based on what they have seen on the television and in films. They tend to -

- be unfamiliar with the language and specialist vocabulary of legal proceedings;
- have little knowledge of the procedures involved and find it difficult to apply the rules even if they do read them;
- lack objectivity and emotional distance from their case;
- be unskilled in advocacy and unable to undertake cross-examination or test the evidence of an opponent;
- be ill-informed about the presentation of evidence;
- be unable to understand the relevance of law and regulations to their own problem, or to know how to challenge a decision that they believe is wrong.

All these factors are likely to have an adverse effect on the preparation and presentation of a litigant in person's case. Litigants in person may also face a daunting range of problems of both knowledge and understanding arising from the following issues –

(i) English or Welsh may not be the first language of the litigant in person and they may have particular difficulties with written English or Welsh. Any papers received from the court or from other parties may therefore need to be translated. A mutually acceptable interpreter may be required to attend the proceedings to explain to the litigant in person in their own language what is taking place, and to assist in the translation of evidence and submissions. This issue would need to be dealt with in advance at the Case Management Conference (CMC).

(ii) Litigants in person come from a variety of social and educational backgrounds. Some may have difficulty with reading, writing and spelling. Advocates should therefore be sensitive to literacy problems and be prepared where possible to agree short adjournments to allow a litigant more time to read or to ask anyone accompanying the litigant to help them to read and understand documents.

(iii) Litigants in person need to be informed at an early stage that they must prove what they say by witness evidence so may need to approach witnesses in advance and ask them to come to court and that no party can call an expert witness unless permission has been given by the court in advance.

(iv) Litigants in person may phrase questions wrongly and some find it hard not to make a statement when they should be cross-examining. In these circumstances the judge may need to explain the difference between evidence and submissions, and help them put across a point in question form. Litigants in person may also have difficulty in understanding that merely because there is a different version of events to their own, this does not necessarily mean that the other side is lying. Similarly, they may construe any suggestion from the other side that their own version is not true as an accusation of lying.

(v) Some useful material for litigants in person and those professionals required to interact with them is available as follows:

    a. Guidance for Litigants in Person released in June 2015 by The Bar Council, CILEx and The Law Society - Litigants in Person Guidance[39]

    b. The Handbook for Litigants in Person[40]:

    c. Report on access to justice for Litigants in Person[41]

    d. A literature review of published research on litigants in person in civil and family courts[42]:

    e. Judicial College Equal Treatment Bench Book, Litigants in Person (November 2013) and associated practice direction[43]

    f. The Personal Support Unit. Part funded by The Ministry of Justice, PSU provides free, independent, practical and emotional support for litigants in person facing civil court proceedings[44].

    g. Lawworks is a pro bono representatives group currently working in partnership with The Personal Support Unit to set up new clinics under a 'Secondary Specialisation Scheme,'

---

[39] Law Society Guidance on Litigants in Person http://www.lawsociety.org.uk/support-services/advice/articles/litigants-in-person-new-guidelines-for-lawyers-june-2015/

[40] Judiciary guidance on Litigants in Person https://www.judiciary.gov.uk/wp content/uploads/JCO/Documents/Guidance/A_Hand book_for_Litigants _in_Person.pdf

[41] Judiciary Report on Litigants in Person https://www.judiciary.gov.uk/wp-content/uploads/2014/05/report-on-access-to-justice-for-litigants-in-person-nov2011.pdf

[42] Government data on Litigants in Person < https://www.gov.uk/government/uploads/system/uploads/attachment_data/file/2173 74/litigants-in-pers on-literature-review.pdf >

[43] Judicial College guidance on Litigants in person https://www.judiciary.gov.uk/wp-content/uploads/JCO/Documents/judicial-college/ETBB_LiP+_finalised_.pdf

[44] PSU guidance for Litigants in person https:// *www.thepsu.org*

which is part funded by the Ministry of Justice. Law firms, with specialist training, will take on case handling on a pro bono basis for litigants in person[45].

CONCLUSION

Toolkit 17 did not deal with the issue of capacity in detail. However, representatives, advocates and judges must ensure that identification and assessment of capacity is undertaken with consideration of what measures may enable effective participation so that vulnerable people are not incorrectly excluded from conducting their own proceedings. In the end, it comes to this: Courts are also daunting and unfriendly places, where very personal issues, often traumatic to the individual concerned, are ventilated. Advocates and the judiciary in criminal cases are changing the way they practice to recognise that it is incumbent on a system of justice to protect the vulnerable and disadvantaged. Research as set out by The Advocate's Gateway has demonstrated that trials involving vulnerable witnesses and suspects need to be approached in a developmentally appropriate and effective way by all parties and the judiciary. This applies throughout the trial in any justice system. Proper presentation of cases involving vulnerable people involves the provisions of special measures which might include; picture boards for witnesses with limited communication; or signers for deaf defendants; or pre-recorded video interviews for children giving evidence. Balance and fairness must be maintained without loss of dignity or respect. Toolkit 17 on advocacy with vulnerable witnesses and parties in civil courts is a step towards achieving this in the civil justice system.

---

[45] Law Works Clinics Information: www.lawworks.org.uk/clinics.

Making Special Measures Special: Reasonable Adjustments for Deaf Witnesses and Defendants

DR. SUE O' ROURKE
Clinical Psychologist and Sign Language Interpreter

CLARE WADE
Criminal Barrister Garden Court Chambers

This article aims to assist in the case management and in the conduct of cases which involve deaf witnesses and defendants.

The issues raised below concern people who are born deaf or become deaf early in life, who rely predominantly on Sign Language. Individuals who are deafened later in life, after the acquisition of speech, including older adults, have their own different needs, relating to the acoustic environment rather than linguistic differences, which are beyond the scope of this article. Guidance for lawyers working with a range of deaf people can be found at (The Advocates Gateway website) *Toolkit number 11 Planning to Question Someone who is Deaf.* [1]

Although there are around 70,000 deaf sign language users in the UK and British Sign Language (BSL), since 2005, has become an officially recognised language[2], most hearing people have not met a deaf person and are not familiar with BSL, other than perhaps seeing occasional TV interpretation. It follows then that most legal professionals will not have experience in working with deaf clients.

Whilst the medical model defines deafness in terms of impairment, the social model defines the Deaf Community as a social, linguistic and cultural minority with its own language and social norms. This contrasts with the

---

[1] www.theadvocatesgateway.org/toolkits
[2] Office for Disability Issues : http://odi.dwp.gov.uk/inclusive-communications/alternative-formats/british-sign-language.php

medical model, which focusses on compensating for deficits; assisting the deaf person to become as 'hearing' as possible. The preferred model of the Deaf Community focuses less on issues of 'impairment' and more on the appropriate steps the hearing world needs to take to ensure access for deaf people, accepting deafness as a difference rather than something which needs to be cured.

Assumptions are often made about deafness and deaf people. The most common assumption is that of incompetence. This has strong historical roots in the denial of sign language as a language; language was equated with thought, and speech with language – ergo no speech no thought! Deaf people were therefore assumed to be unintelligent and incapable of thinking. Although this extreme position is no longer held, the vestiges of this view can be seen in misunderstandings about sign language being a 'concrete' or 'basic' language, inferior to spoken language or in assumptions that individual deaf people are learning disabled. A review of all medico-legal cases referred to a psychiatric services, found a large proportion of referrals were for an opinion on fitness to plead, often when the individual had no cognitive impairment, suggesting assumptions of incompetence persist.[3] In the first author's own experience, in situations when the deaf person appears to struggle with understanding proceedings, the difficulty is often assumed to lie in cognitive limitations of the deaf person, rather than in the complexity of the legal system.

It is true that within the Deaf Community there is a subgroup of individuals with additional difficulties, associated with their cause of deafness, this includes those with intellectual impairment. There are also deaf people who, though of average intellectual potential, have suffered terrible deprivation of language and learning and therefore function as if intellectually impaired. However, there are also deaf people who are professors and academics, psychologists, engineers and business people.

COMMUNICATION

In order to consider deaf people in legal proceedings, it is important to have an understanding of communication issues and in particular, British Sign Language.

British Sign Language (BSL) is the natural sign language of the Deaf community in Britain. It is not a gestural representation of English and has its own grammatical structure with a word order different from spoken English. In legal settings, the assumption that word-for-sign translation is

---

[3] Alys Young, Paul Howarth, Sharon Ridgeway & Brendan Monteiro "Forensic referrals to the three specialist psychiatric units for deaf people in the UK" The Journal of Forensic Psychiatry (2001) Volume 12 Issue 1 19-35.

possible or desirable is often the cause of much confusion and delay in proceedings, as arguments arise about the exact nature of the interpretation, borne out of a misunderstanding of the role. There are regional accents and dialects in BSL much like any spoken language and it is dynamic, changing and developing in the same way as a spoken language. It is not the same as American Sign Language, Irish Sign Language, French Sign Language and so forth.

It is commonly believed that BSL is very concrete and struggles to communicate abstract concepts. This is not the case; the language is not impoverished but unfortunately many deaf people have impoverished developmental experiences and their ability to communicate abstract concepts is limited, not the language *per se*.

BSL is a visual language created in three dimensional space as opposed to spoken English which is verbal. In this article we refer to this dichotomy between the visual and the verbal as 'bi-modality'. The result of this difference is that some matters which are easily spoken in English are not easily interpreted in BSL. In other situations a longwinded and laborious sentence in English can be communicated in BSL in just a few signs. As is the case for spoken languages, interpretation involves some degree of 'cultural mediation'[4] whereby the source language is transformed, not literally, but in a culturally appropriate way, into the target language. A simple example may be that in BSL the use of sign names or initials to indicate a person is acceptable, even in a formal setting such as a court; an English interpretation of 'the man with the fat belly with glasses' or even 'MS' is not acceptable and would be translated as 'Mr Smith' provided of course that the interpreter was aware of the identity of the deaf person described in this manner.

The unit of interpretation is not the individual word or even phrase, but meaning. This often leads to further confusion in a legal setting, as counsel measure each word carefully, only to have it reduced to the core meaning, or repeat a question using different words in the attempt to assist, when the interpretation of two questions with the same meaning will in fact be the same.

Written Information: It is often wrongly assumed that in the absence of hearing, information can be written down in order to communicate. Although there are deaf people with good facility in English, this is often not the case for two reasons. First, English is the second language of most deaf people who use BSL. While a deaf person may be able to read simple information, increasing complexity leads to increased unreliability as the vocabulary is unfamiliar and the structure of English is not the same as the

---

[4] Stewart DA, Schein JD and Cartwright BE *Sign Language Interpreting: Exploring its Art and Science*. Allyn &Bacon (2004).

structure of BSL. In particular, legal documents and reports are likely to be misunderstood. Secondly, due to often poor educational opportunities, even for deaf people of average and above intelligence, the English in such documents is impenetrable. Research indicates that the average reading age of a deaf school leaver is around 7-9 years.[5] Written information along the lines of 'appointment Friday 2pm' is fine, giving a deaf client a long and complex report or statement is not. This requires interpretation into BSL. Best practice would be to video record interpretation of key documents in order that the deaf person can refer back to them. Although time consuming, this would be provide equality of access to information.

FREQUENTLY USED SPECIAL MEASURES

Provision of Interpreters: Interpreters are independent professionals, regulated by NRCPD[6] and who operate within a professional code of practice. All interpreters in legal proceedings should be fully qualified, registered and have experience in this domain. All pre-trial interviews and meetings require a BSL interpreter, separate from the ones employed in court, and other professionals, family and friends should never be used as a 'cheap' or convenient option since they are neither qualified nor impartial.[7]

Interpreting is a complex task which makes considerable cognitive demands on the interpreter. For this reason, interpreters in court work ideally in a team of three; one person working, a second assisting and the third resting, rotating about every 30 minutes. Interpreting is not an exact process. It is a constant matter of selecting from a range of possible lexical choices in both languages; do I say very angry or furious? walking slowly or strolling?, very hungry or starving? All of these choices, although they arguably mean the same thing in essence, can affect the impression given of a defendant or witness in court. This suggests the need for monitoring of the interpreting process. In addition, an interpreter who is hesitant or asks for clarification can give the impression that the deaf person is uncertain, when in fact it is a difficulty in interpretation. The role of the interpreter is to 'reflect' the deaf person; this adds information about mood and manner which is important to the court, but the impression gained is dependent on the skill of the interpreter and their characteristics. Occasionally, the interpreter will simply not understand the deaf person; this may reflect that the deaf person is in fact difficult to understand for reasons which

---

[5] Maybery R (2002) "Cognitive development in deaf children: The interface of language and perception in neuropsychology". *Handbook of Neuropsychology* Eds Segalowitz S & Rapin I 2nd ed, vol 8 pt II pp 71-107.
[6] The National Registers of Communication Professionals working with Deaf and Deafblind People.
[7] See *Re C (A Child) (Care Proceedings) Practice Note* [2014] EWCA (Civ) 128.

may be deliberate or reflect disability. Alternatively, it may be an issue of interpretation which is presenting as hesitancy. In this instance the court needs advice in order to proceed.

The nature of interpreting means that there are always likely to be errors, or differences in opinion regarding how a particular matter should be interpreted. These may be minor and unimportant or major with huge evidential implications for the case.

Provision of Relays: Deaf people with minimal language skills due to Learning Disability or deprivation may benefit from the services of a Deaf Relay. This is a deaf person, usually someone who works with deaf people who have additional difficulties. The Deaf Relay works with the interpreters to assist communication, for example by adding clarifying information or using examples. Such additions should be sanctioned by the court at the time of interpretation.

Provision of Intermediaries: Ministry of Justice Registered Intermediaries (RI's) are employed to improve access to justice for vulnerable witnesses[8] and may be involved throughout the legal process, with a key role in assisting effective communication[9].

There are a number of deaf RI's working with deaf witnesses in court. The advantage of employing a deaf RI is that his or her first language is BSL and he or she is therefore likely to be able to understand idiosyncratic or limited BSL. Ideally, the Intermediary (registered or otherwise) is able to work with the deaf defendant or witness throughout the process, for example from police interview or ABE to proceedings. He or she therefore can develop a rapport and crucially, understanding, regarding language. By way of example, this may include signs for certain people, the best ways to communicate time, how to deal with specific concepts which are complex or traumatic. In court the deaf RI works with the interpreters, who will have no prior knowledge of the deaf person other than a brief 'rapport' meeting, to assist communication. Often the role of the deaf RI encompasses the role of a Deaf Relay which, although arguably providing considerable assistance to the court, raises other issues and concerns which are discussed below.

---

[8] Deaf defendants have access to an unregistered intermediary. In practice, there are very few deaf intermediaries.
[9] Criminal Justice and Youth Evidence Act 1999 section 29(2) The function of an intermediary is to communicate-
    (a)   to the witness, questions put to the witness, and
    (b)   to any person asking such questions, the answers given by the witness in reply to them
and to explain such questions or answers so far as necessary to enable them to be understood by the witness or person in question.

SPECIAL MEASURES AND THE TRIAL PROCESS

There is no doubt that in a modern, fair and effective criminal justice system there must be accessibility for all participants (whether witnesses or defendants) whilst maintaining transparency and the integrity of the trial process. When dealing with very young children as witnesses and the question of their competence, the courts have adopted a pragmatic stance which involves making adjustments to cross-examination.[10] Whereas this has become an accepted method of accommodating the vulnerable witness within the trial process[11], there is a danger that without further analysis, special measures will not get the consideration they deserve. Pragmatism on the part of the courts is not a reason for policy makers to disregard the practical difficulties which are likely to ensue if attention is not paid to the need to balance measures with specific questions of fairness and to think through the way in which any measures may affect the adduction of evidence or the quality of that evidence.

SPECIAL MEASURES AND DEAFNESS

The tension caused by the competing interests of reasonable adjustments and fairness in an adversarial system is as much, if not more, apparent in the hitherto little explored area of deafness as in other areas of vulnerability or special needs. Despite deaf people appearing in court and the provision of professional interpreters, legal professionals have no training in working with this client group.

Although the Deaf Community rail against the notion that deafness is a disability, identifying themselves as a cultural and linguistic minority, we would suggest that the courts need to take account of the needs of deaf people beyond the provision of interpreters and sometimes intermediaries. This is because of the clear and complex 'culture clash' between the highly specialised English language based process of proceedings and the workings of a visuo-spatial language. The court room has often been cited as providing the most complex forum for interaction between those whose first language is English and those who use BSL.[12]

---

[10] *R v B* [2010] *EWCA Crim* 4 at [42] "Aspects of evidence which undermine or are believed to undermine the child's credibility must, of course, be revealed to the jury but it is not necessarily appropriate to form the subject matter of detailed cross-examination of the child and the advocate may have to forego much of the kind of contemporary cross-examination which consists of no more than comment on matters which will be before the jury in any event from different sources."

[11] *R v Wills* (Practice Note) [2012] 1 Cr. App.R 2.

[12] Graham H Turner "The bilingual, bimodal courtroom: a first glance." In Interpreting Interpreting: Studies and reflections on sign language interpreting eds Harrington FJ & Turner GH. Douglas McClean.

Regardless of level of ability, accommodating the needs of deaf people in court is a challenge; one which becomes increasingly complex in cases where the deaf person has additional needs.

Assumptions in relation to impaired cognitive ability can lead to a pre-trial failure to examine cognitive ability and the premature conclusion that there is a problem with competence or fitness. In the first author's experience a consequence of erroneous assumptions regarding intellectual ability sometimes manifests itself as a reluctance to prosecute deaf individuals, assuming they will be unfit to plead or that the process will be too costly and time-consuming.

At the other end of the spectrum, an implicit medical model of deafness leads to assumptions that deaf people merely have 'broken ears' and once this is fixed by using written information or a sign language interpreter, the court can proceed untroubled. This view fuels a resistance to specific special measures as it fails to take into account the developmental experiences of deaf people, culture and language and sees the individual as 'just deaf'.

In fact, the real focus of attention and adaptation should be the linguistic challenges which are inherent in the bi-modal courtroom.

Given the competence test[13] (which requires that a witness be able to understand questions and give answers which can be understood) and that aspect of the *Pritchard* test (which requires that a defendant be able to follow the proceedings)[14], there is every reason to investigate a deaf person's ability with the assistance of specialists. In *R v F (JR)*[15] the Court of Appeal found a competence hearing to have been flawed. The court at first instance had proceeded with a competence hearing in the case of a complainant who was profoundly deaf and who was said to have learning disabilities, with the assistance of a deaf RI and a sign language interpreter. The Court of Appeal held that the court had prematurely and erroneously found that the witness was not competent and notwithstanding the difficulties,[16] the court should have continued to hear the case until half time. Although the Court of Appeal concluded that an RI and a sign language interpreter were sufficient by way of special measures, it is suggested that the court at first instance would have been assisted by a psychologist with an expertise in British Sign Language because he or she would have enabled the questioning to be adapted to the cognitive ability of the witness. As we observe below, an intermediary can comment on understanding but cannot offer an expert opinion on the cause of a lack of understanding.

---

[13] See s 53 (3) Youth Justice and Criminal Evidence Act 1999.
[14] *R v Pritchard* (above) and *R V Davies* (1853) Car & Kir 328 and *M (John)* [2003] EWCA Crim 3452 at [22] and [23].
[15] [2013] 2 Cr. App. R. 13.
[16] The witness was said to have no understanding of time and could only express what the defendant had been alleged to have done by pointing to pictures of body parts.

If this issue is not addressed at an early stage, problems can become apparent during the trial. Frequently, deaf people appear to struggle with aspects of the legal process even when provided with a sign language interpreter. This then tends to lead to the often erroneous view that the deaf person is cognitively impaired. However, many deaf people with average intellectual ability, through lack of access to information and learning which is normally acquired incidentally by hearing people, may arrive at adulthood with significant gaps in their general knowledge.[17] What the court is faced with is deprivation of learning and lack of knowledge which may in some cases be accommodated by providing clear, jargon-free explanation and extra time for questions and explanation. However, too often the courts assume the problem resides within the deaf person themselves rather than the complexity of the system which is either trying them or receiving their evidence. Non-specialist assessment can compound the difficulties; psychiatrists and psychologists without knowledge of deafness and BSL can equally fall prey to assumptions; misdiagnosis of learning disability and lack of capacity are not uncommon.

In light of the above, particular attention should be given to the question of providing for an early specialist psychological assessment. If a deaf RI is involved, his or her assessment will comment on communication, but will be unable to point to the cause of difficulties, see *R v F (JR)* [18] where, we suggest, the deaf RI could help the court to some extent but could not offer an opinion on the cause or extent of the cognitive difficulty. As with hearing defendants, specific consideration should obviously be given to the possibility of mental illness or learning disability. Assessment of cognitive ability of a deaf person is a highly specialised area of clinical psychology. Although some hearing intermediaries are psychologists, they are not able to work with deaf people as this is outside their remit. Currently no deaf intermediaries are also trained as psychologists and therefore the ability of RIs to carry out assessment in this respect is limited. Without specialist assessment, it is easier to overlook such conditions in the case of deaf defendants than it is in the case of hearing defendants. Conversely, it is easy to misjudge cognitive abilities which may not be readily apparent, making an assumption of incompetence.

Once specialist cognitive assessments have taken place (in the case of a defendant), it may be necessary to consider issues of fitness to plead. A true deficit of language by virtue of the difficulties which we have outlined

---

[17] See Vernon MacCay and Andrews Jean "Basic Legal issues in handling the cases of deaf defendants." The Champion March 2011 at p 30 where it is pointed out that "deafness has… severe impacts on language, communication, learning and socialisation [which are often not acknowledged]."

[18] [2013] 2 Cr,.App,.R. 13.

in the paragraphs below could mean that a deaf person's disability is such that he or she is not in a position to follow proceedings in court.[19] In *Re C (A Child)*[20] the Court of Appeal (Civil Division) emphasised the importance of early assessment and the provision of funding for this as being an essential case-management issue.[21] In that case, care proceedings were determined against parents at first instance because the father who was profoundly deaf was not interviewed through a BSL interpreter but with the assistance of his wife who was hearing but had a mild learning disability. It was assumed by all that he had given informed consent to an order under section 20 of the Children Act 1989. When interviewed by a BSL qualified psychologist for the purpose of appeal proceedings, he was found to be of 'significant intelligence to degree level.'[22]

It is necessary to examine the impact of deafness on issues of communication and understanding. It has been claimed that bi-modal dynamics (the effect of the process of interpreting from BSL to a verbal language and vice versa) are poorly understood by 'most of the major players in the court room'[23] and have even at times gone 'unrecognised' by deaf people and interpreters themselves.[24]

Our assertion is that the courts require a fundamental shift to understand the difficulties faced by deaf people in proceedings and need to adapt proceedings to take this into account, including in these adaptations training for advocates and the judiciary

It is easy to assume that the only necessary adaptation of the court process is the provision of a British Sign Language (BSL) interpreter[25] but as MacKay and Andrews have made clear, 'nothing could be further from the truth'.[26] There are a number of further issues which arise from differences

---

[19] In which case or she would not be fit to plead. See *R v M (John)* [2003] EWCA Crim 3452 at [20] where it was held that an inability to follow any one of the Pritchard criteria means that a defendant is unfit to plead.
[20] [2014] EWCA Civ 128.
[21] Above at [18]-[20]. [24]-[27], [37] and [38].
[22] Above at [11].
[23] Mary Brennan and Richard Brown *Equality before the Law. Deaf people's access to justice* (2004) Douglas McLean 118.
[24] Brennan and Brown (above) 118.
[25] Graham H Turner "The bilingual, bimodal courtroom: a first glance." In Interpreting Interpreting: Studies and reflections on sign language interpreting eds Harrington FJ & Turner GH. Douglas McClean. at p 128.
[26] Maccay Vernon and Jean Andrews (above) *Basic Legal issues in handling the cases of deaf defendants* The Champion March 2011 at p 30 who refer to the limitations of American Sign Language when compared to English "Sign language is a highly expressive and fascinating language, but it has some severe limitations. One such limitation is the vocabulary: the largest commercially available dictionary of ASL has only 5.600 signs. By contrast the *Shorter Oxford English Dictionary* has over half a million words."

in language and culture which are not readily apparent to those who are not bilingual.[27]

BSL/English interpreters are not only working between two different languages but have to work within distinct modalities and engage in some degree of cultural brokerage in terms of how language is used and constructed. The often heard request from the judiciary or practitioners to 'just sign everything that is being said' belies a lack of understanding of the nature of the interpretation process.[28] This is a situation which can be misconceived by lawyers, judges and other professionals.[29] BSL involves placing a visual perspective on events and how that is done in any particular scenario, will depend on context. By way of illustration and as Brennan and Brown state, there are many BSL signs which represent the English word 'murder,' depending on how the murder was committed.[30] Since a sign has to have a shape and exist in three dimensional space, murder by stabbing, or beating or shooting must appear very different in BSL. Similarly, BSL signs may have a number of possible interpretations in English and the interpreter has to make continual lexical choices. The choice of sign/word on the part of an interpreter will depend on his or her understanding of the relevant context. Further, what is referred to by Turner[31] as 'visual ambiguity in the English wording' is often confronted (on the part of signers) by offering a series of visual alternatives in BSL.[32]

To take a hypothetical example:

Barrister: did you or did you not have a weapon?

---

[27] In spoken English and BSL.
[28] Graham H Turner "The bilingual, bimodal courtroom: a first glance." In Intepreting Interpreting: Studies and reflections on sign language interpreting eds Harrington FJ & Turner GH. Douglas McClean. at p 128.
at p128 "such an instruction serves only to underline (a) the court's lack of awareness of, or trust in, interpreting procedures and (b) a lack of appreciation of what must occur in the very process of interpreting".
[29] See Turner (above) at p129 citing Butler and Nooks (1992) where it was suggested that such professionals tended to assume that interpretation "is an entirely mechanical task requiring negligible analytical skills".
[30] Mary Brennan and Richard Brown *Equality before the Law. Deaf people's access to justice* (2004) Douglas McLean at p123.
[31] Graham H Turner "The bilingual, bimodal courtroom: a first glance." In Intepreting Interpreting: Studies and reflections on sign language interpreting eds Harrington FJ & Turner GH. Douglas McClean. at p138.
[32] Turner (above) at p138, he gives the example of the interpretation of the English question "How did you get into the factory grounds?" might take the signed form more literally equivalent to " Did you get into the factory grounds by climbing over the wall through a window, breaking in the door or what". In other words the question is altered during the interpretation process.

Interpreter: could you clarify what type of weapon we are referring to?

Barrister: No, I just want to ask the general question – surely there is a sign for weapon?

Intepreter: erm... well not really, but I will try. <BEFORE (indicating earlier in time) YOU HAD W-E-A-P-O-N, YES OR NO?> (finger spelling weapon)

Defendant: <WHAT? DUNNO>

Interpreter: I am sorry your honour, I have spelt the word weapon and he doesn't understand, can I give examples?

Judge: yes go ahead

Interpreter: <BEFORE YOU HAVE KNIFE?GUN?BAT? > :

Defendant: <NO>

Interpreter: No I didn't have a weapon

In these circumstances, it is not difficult to see how a witness may be led into giving a particular answer or conversely, how the court can be misled over the absence of the answer which is sought. Further, the translation procedure means that there are potential problems in terms of accuracy of statements which may not be appreciated at first blush. In terms of involvement there will often be sign language interpreters and a deaf RI. Arguably, the more people involved in the process, then the greater the possibility of there being changes between the source language and the target language. Interpreters or other persons charged with assisting communication are in reality, changing language at a number of stages and if the 'hearing' court is unaware of the difficulties involved in the process of bi-modal translation then there is a capacity for error and/ or misunderstanding.

Such changes as inevitably occur may have a significance within the legal process which is concerned with the question of 'why' as much as it is concerned with the 'who,' 'what,' 'where' and 'when'. At its most extreme, this can lead to unreliability, particularly if the process happens without the court being alive to the dangers. This is a factor which has been recognised by experts.[33]

As stated earlier, asking the deaf defendant or witness to read legal documents and statements is likely to be unrealistic. The court needs to appreciate that English is, for many deaf people, a second language. This (coupled with difficulties in accessing education for many deaf people) means that it is likely that all written material therefore requires interpretation into BSL.[34] A problem which has been identified by commentators within the specialist literature is caused by the fact that, 'written statements, based on verbatim records of spoken utterances, play a large part in courts...this means that courts are not particularly comfortable with languages without a written form. British Sign Language is such a language. The courts still require BSL to be pinned down in written form and the only way in which this is currently possible or acceptable is through written English. This is always and inevitably at least twice removed from the original, i.e. it involves translation into another language, in a different modality, and then a further modality change from spoken to written'.[35]

As Brennan and Brown go on to point out, this causes problems 'in every part of the process yet, little account seems to be taken of this within the court room'.[36]

Court proceedings are audio recorded so as to produce an oral and written record of examination-in-chief, cross-examination and re-examination but this does not assist with the production of an accurate record of that evidence which is given in BSL as the audio recording is not the original evidence. Further, there is a very obvious difficulty in the fact that if there is a dispute as to what has been said at a particular time (by virtue of what sign has been used or how a particular sign has been voiced by the interpreter) then it is not possible for the court to return to the evidence to check it. Neither can there be any proper peer review of the interpreting process or challenges brought by either side. Whereas an audio recording of a spoken language interpretation can be replayed and checked, there is no facility to do this with BSL interpretation and the

---

[33] See Turner (above) at p132 citing Berk Seligson (1990:178) "if interpretation renders the message more or less fragmented than the original utterance, it has altered the effect of what was signed or said. Such alterations though their effects may not be immediately apparent, are unlikely to be inconsequential, particularly when they accumulate throughout the duration of a section of testimony".

[34] The average reading age of a deaf school leaver is around 8-9 years. Maybery R (2002)" Cognitive development in deaf children: The interface of language and perception in neuropsychology" Segalowitz S & Rapin I (Eds) *Handbook of Neuropsychology* 2nd ed, vol 8 pt II pp 71-107.

[35] Mary Brennan and Richard Brown *Equality before the Law. Deaf people's access to justice* (2004) Douglas McLean p120.

[36] Brennan and Brown (above) p120.

original evidence in BSL is lost, as is the exact nature of the interpretation of questions from English into BSL It is our contention that without a video-recording of the deaf person's evidence in court, neither the deaf person nor the court are protected in this regard, as the interpretation of what has been said by the witness cannot be challenged. This immediately distinguishes 'deaf' cases from other cases which require the deployment of special measures. In *R v IA, TA and FA*[37] the Court of Appeal was left without a proper record of that aspect of the proceedings which concerned cross-examination. The Court did not see the failure to visually record cross-examination as a problem but did not provide any reason as to why it should not be necessary for a record of what is said visually as much as what is said orally. Neither did the court address the issue that there was no recording of the original evidence given by the deaf person in cross-examination or of the interpretation into BSL.[38] It is important to note however that in this case, it was only the absence of the availability of the required facilities which prevented the trial judge from implementing the measure.

A contrasting approach was taken with success in the Snaresbrook Crown Court in *R v H and another* in June 2014. This was a complex case involving multiple deaf witnesses and deaf defendants. It also involved the translation from American Sign Language into British Sign Language. One issue of concern was the failure to visually record the interpreter in the ABE, therefore not permitting any comment or challenge of how the questions were actually interpreted. The judge was alive to this issue and ruled that, if the practicalities could be overcome, visual recording of evidence in court would be permitted. The court funded and was greatly assisted by Remark! a deaf media company, who provided a camera person. Each day the recordings of the evidence were downloaded to DVD, sealed and signed, by the officer in the case and counsel. The recordings were then kept on the court file. The deaf participants were content with the recording and reassured that they would be able to challenge interpretation if they wished to. In fact, the ability to challenge was straightforward, occurring rarely and, given the availability of the recording, all concerned accepted they had made errors when these occurred, with little debate. It is suggested that, in addition to allowing recording of the evidence, which protects the legal process, this method inadvertently went some way to redress the

---

[37] [2013] EWCA Crim 1308.
[38] See *R v IA, TA and FA* (above) at [64]. Cross-examination was conducted with assistance from a BSL fluent psychologist who had assessed the witness's cognitive abilities and who advised on the modification of language. A point which may have been apparent had there been a visual recording. Any such advice would have been apparent from the ground rules hearing agreement, or from the transcript. This sort of discussion between a court-appointed expert and counsel does not happen without being reflected in the court record in some way.

power imbalance often felt by deaf people in court, again assisted by the presence of a deaf cameraman.

Other accommodations in this case included allowing a deaf defendant into the well of the court while a deaf co-defendant was giving evidence in order that the defendant had a better view of the signing. Further, there was a recognition on the part of the legal professionals involved that in cases where there is a deaf defendant, it is preferable for a witness to give evidence over a live link as opposed to being present in court and giving evidence from behind a screen. This is because the deaf defendant cannot hear what is being said and is deprived of a first-hand appreciation of the evidence against him.

The use of video recording provides a true record of the evidence which can be reviewed; but how would a challenge occur, since the deaf people involved have no access to English and the hearing people are unable to understand BSL?

Where a witness called on behalf of one party to the proceedings requires a registered qualified sign language interpreter, it is essential that provision should be made for the other side to have access to an interpreter in order to monitor the interpretation which is being conducted.[39] This is not to suggest that the interpretation of a qualified professional is 'wrong' but rather an acknowledgement of the complexity of the task and the fact that in any interpretation, there are lexical choices to be made which can alter the meaning or impression given by evidence, errors always occur and important information may be missed. This is all the more important if evidence is not video-recorded.

It is becoming more common to employ a Deaf Relay, in addition to a sign language interpreter particularly, when the deaf person has minimal language skills and/or a learning disability. There are issues in using a deaf relay in a legal setting. First, it is currently an unregulated role with no specific or standardised training, although training courses exist. Secondly, the extent to which the Relay alters the source language to convey it in the target language is not transparent to, or controlled by the court. This can have serious implications and again this points to the need for video recording and monitoring of communication in court.

The inevitable 'adding in' information to the question to make it clearer may be necessary and wholly appropriate but there is a danger that it may not reflect the intention of the questioner. Again, this points to the need for video recording in order that proper challenges to this process are possible.

---

[39] In a study conducted by Brennan and Brown 39 out of 67 BSL interpreters who were employed to interpret for the court reported that they had been asked to interpret between a defendant/ and his or her legal team. Mary Brennan and Richard Brown *Equality before the Law. Deaf people's access to justice* (2004) Douglas McLean.

The situation has developed whereby a deaf RI often subsumes the role of the Deaf Relay. Whilst the use of an interpreter, Deaf Relay and RI may appear unnecessarily complex and lead to confusion, there are concerns about the merging of roles. It is important not to confuse the role of an RI with that of a Deaf Relay.[40] They do different jobs which are not mutually consistent. The intermediary is employed to monitor and assist understanding 'where necessary'.[41] A Deaf Relay will communicate all information, and neither a Deaf Relay nor an RI are supposed to change the meaning of what is said.[42] Both however may 'add' information to assist understanding. In this, the RI has the advantage in assisting communication, having been present at pre-proceedings interviews, becoming familiar with idiosyncratic signs and the person's history and evidence. The Deaf Relay has no such familiarity and is in a similar situation to the court interpreters. Arguably the RI is better equipped to assist, but in this situation, what of the ability of the RI to monitor the interpretation process? How, in this case, is the interpretation process entirely independent and free from possible bias or 'contamination'? If the roles of the Deaf Relay and the RI are conflated then arguably the integrity of the trial process is jeopardised.[43] This is because if the RI is acting as a Deaf Relay, he or she cannot undertake the monitoring function and, we would argue, becomes part of the interpreting team. Furthermore, since the result of using a Deaf Relay or an RI can be to inadvertently 'tidy up' dysfluent language to preserve meaning, there is a danger that the deaf person can appear more sensible, clear and able than is the case.[44] In the normal course of events, it would be the role of the RI to alert the court to the process and difficulties; something he or she cannot do at the same time as being the Deaf Relay. In short, in our view the RI cannot alert the court to the risks of the interpreting process while he or she is part of that process. A consequence of this is that it may lead to a false sense of competence which the court is not in a position to appreciate.

Although there are advantages to employing a deaf RI as a first language BSL user and while it would seem self-evident that an RI who is

---

[40] *R v IA, TA and FA* (above) at [36] the Court of Appeal did not address the distinction between relay and intermediary and the fact that the former changes language while the latter monitors understanding and intervenes if necessary.

[41] Criminal Justice and Youth Evidence Act section 29(2)(b).

[42] The Registered Intermediary Procedural Guidance Manual (2012) Part 3 The Registered Intermediary Code of Practice and the Registered Intermediary Code of Ethics at 15 "[the Registered Intermediary] must not change the content of what is being said or attempt to improve or elaborate what has been said".

[43] The purpose of the trial process is to ascertain what evidence is reliable and what is not. In our view, this requires that everything is transparent to the hearing court.

[44] Sue O'Rourke, Neil Glickman and Sally Austen Deaf People in the Criminal Justice System: "Is A Culturally Affirmative Response Possible or Desirable?" In *Deaf Mental Health Care*, (Ed) Glickman N (2013).

not fluent in BSL cannot perform his or her role, it should be borne in mind that where a deaf RI is being used, then he or she does not have access to the original questions asked in court or to the voice over which is being given by the interpreter. Any evidence which is given by a deaf person, and transcribed by audio-taping the voice of an interpreter, would need to be reduced to written English and then checked by the deaf RI in order for the RI to confirm if this was his or her understanding of the evidence. Alternatively and more immediately, the deaf RI has his or her own sign language interpreter who provides a back translation of the interpreters' English voice-over in order that he or she knows what is being said. The deaf RI also may not have a good facility in English for the same reason as the deaf witness/defendant may not have it, and so for him or her, any English written information, including transcripts of evidence may need to be back translated into BSL. The complexities involved in the process are self-evident. This has particular relevance to statements or accounts which are given before a hearing i.e. at the investigation stage. If this is not done, then there are likely to be disputes (about what was said previously) within the course of the adduction of evidence at trial. Disputes will arise during cross-examination if for example, an ABE voice over has not been back translated and checked by the Deaf RI. Accordingly, in the case of a severe linguistic deficit and where a deaf RI has been used in the police station either for the conducting of an ABE interview or for the interview of a suspect, then he or she should check and verify the written record of what the interpreter has said was said, before the trial.

The complexities involved in the use of sign language interpreters, Deaf RIs and Deaf Relays are clear; we would argue that further consideration of the impact of these difficulties is required and that special measures for deaf people require special attention to ensure their efficacy and minimise unintended consequences.

The most single important special measure which we suggest could be effected would be to introduce a visual recording of evidence. Given the complexities of interpretation, neither the court or the deaf person are served well by the current situation which does not allow appropriate challenges to the interpretation, because there is no original with which it can be compared. In *R v IA, TA and FA*, challenges to the voice over of the ABE interviews occurred which were resolved at trial by referring to the original interview enabling all parties to comment; in each case there was agreement about elements which had been missed or misinterpreted. As previously stated however, such challenges were not able to be pursued satisfactorily in relation to evidence given at the trial.

'Deaf awareness' training for legal professionals should be considered prior to a case. Training of all the legal professionals involved in a 'deaf case' would allow an understanding of areas of difficulty and pre-empting of issues which arise from interpretation. As a minimum, all those involved should be familiar with the Advocacy Training Council's Toolkit 11: Planning to Question Someone who is Deaf (www.theadvocatesgateway.org/toolkits). Without the knowledge imparted by specific training, issues of interpretation can become the focus of cases involving deaf people and can detract from the general issue. Such training is an extension of the current 'ground rules' requirement in cases involving vulnerable witnesses and special measures. For the importance of following proper practice in dealing with vulnerable defendants and of having ground rules meetings see *R v Dixon*[45] where the Court of Appeal held that there had been a failure to follow the Practice Direction in relation to vulnerable defendants in the case of an eighteen year old who suffered from ADHD, had learning difficulties and was charged with murder. There had been no ground rules meeting and no decision as to the way in which the court's procedures should be adapted.[46] Whereas undertaking such training might take half a day prior to the case, it will save considerable time during the trial. Such training has also been recommended in other contexts.[47]

We have already argued the importance of obtaining specialist advice at the outset of the proceedings for the reasons adumbrated earlier in this article. Where a witness is competent or a defendant is fit to plead, it should be borne in mind that language and cognitive abilities could nevertheless still be an issue. Accordingly, cross-examination of a competent witness should be tailored to take into account the specific cognitive abilities of the witness. The Deaf RI will provide a report in relation to communication, but additional assessment by a specialist Clinical Psychologist will assist in tailoring questions to take account of both deafness and any cognitive deficits. In such a situation, the defence should have access to specialist psychological advice provided by a bilingual psychologist during the cross-examination process. If utilised properly, this will assist the advocate in forming questions which will be understood by the witness and it will also enable the advocate to appreciate the limits of a witness's capacity in a particular situation (in other words, competence) as against the general consequences of bi-modal translation. It is only if questions can be adapted

---

[45] [2013] EWCA Crim 465.
[46] However the Court of Appeal held on the facts (the intermediary was said to have ensured that the defendant had understood all relevant matters) these failures did not render the conviction unsafe.
[47] See for example, J Jacobson with J Talbot, Vulnerable Defendants in the Criminal Courts: a review of provisions for adults and children (Prison Reform Trust 2009) recommendation 4 "Judges and Magistrates should receive training on the range of impairments (including learning disabilities) that defendants can display, the implications of these impairments for the criminal justice process and methods by which vulnerable defendants participation in court proceedings can be enhanced".

in light of answers given (or not given) that decisions as to competence can really be made.

The need for realistic trial estimates cannot be over stated. The time it takes to translate into sign language and back should therefore be taken into account at the PCMH stage. Studies have shown that even with highly select groups for whom interpreting is easy, it takes two to four times longer to interpret something into sign language than it does to interpret from a another non-visual language into English.[48][49] For those with additional needs in relation to understanding, additional time is required to provide explanation and to plan careful questioning.[50]

Finally, it is worth noting that notwithstanding an absence of scrutiny by policy makers, there is no limit on a trial judge's common law power to impose special measures on a trial[51] and to thereby ensure the fairness of the trial process. We would argue that in any case involving profoundly deaf witnesses or defendants that the above recommendations (together with an appreciation of the rationale which underpins them) will enable a court to manage a case while simultaneously balancing the needs of all parties to the proceedings and thereby, maintaining the integrity of the trial process.

---

[48] Vernon MacKay and Andrews Jean "Basic Legal issues in handling the cases of deaf defendants." The Champion March 2011 citing BA Brauer Adequacy of a translation of the MMPI into American Sign Language for use with deaf individuals: Linguistic Equivalency issues, 38 Rehabilitation psychol.247-248 (1995); AG Steinberg, DS Lipton, EA Eckhardt, M. Goldstein & VJ Sullivan , the Diagnostic Interview Schedule For Deaf patients On Interactive Video: A preliminary Investigation 155 Am.J Psychiatry 1603-1604 (1998).

[49] In *IA, TA and FA* (above) the Court of Appeal did not acknowledge this. This may have been in part due to the absence of a recording of the proceedings. The Court of Appeal did note that the cross-examination had taken an exceedingly long time, which they concluded was excessive: [73]. This was because of repetitive cross-examination questions and the use of impermissible comment by defence counsel. The Court of Appeal did explain the process used in court. Note that there was a voir dire lasting 42 days, which is quite extraordinary, to deal with all of the issues pertaining to communication and competence of the complainant.

[50] In *IA, TA and FA* (above) all the cross-examination was planned with the assistance of an expert psychologist who had assessed the cognitive abilities of the witness– another point which was overlooked by the Court.

[51] See *R v H.* (Special Measures) the Times April 15 2003.

How Effective are Judges and Counsel at Facilitating Communication with Vulnerable Persons in a Criminal Trial?

DR. BRENDAN M. O'MAHONY
CJS Psychology, and a Visiting Fellow at the Centre of Forensic Interviewing, Institute of Criminal Justice Studies, University of Portsmouth.

INTRODUCTION

Research has found that vulnerable people are disadvantaged by legal discourse in the court (Kebbell, Hatton, and Johnson 2004). Cross-examination techniques in adversarial judicial systems can confuse vulnerable witnesses (Keane 2012). The Advocacy Training Council develops training programmes to ensure that advocates continue to develop their skills as they progress through their career (*The Advocacy Training Council. Excellence in Advocacy: Training the Trainer* 2015). This paper utilises a case study approach to demonstrate why such continued training and development is essential for advocates. It will be argued that advocates might benefit if given the opportunity to read transcripts of their own cross-examination skills to identify strengths and areas where practice could be developed in the questioning of vulnerable persons. It is also questioned whether the current culture and structure of the legal environment permits, and indeed values, the regular provision of feedback from peers and external professionals.

In the Court of Appeal in 2012 the case of *R v Cox* was examined on the basis that the trial should not have taken place due to the defendant's complex psychiatric difficulties. The central focus of the appeal was the absence of an intermediary for the defendant at trial and whether the care

How Effective are Judges and Counsel at Facilitating Communication

and attention in which the trial judge had approached the communication issues was satisfactory in the absence of an intermediary. Registered Intermediaries are communication specialists who are tasked with facilitating communication between vulnerable witnesses and police interviewing officers or counsel at court (*Intermediaries: Step by Step* 2015). Registered Intermediaries are currently not allocated to vulnerable defendants and anyone taking on the intermediary function with a vulnerable defendant does so outside of the Ministry of Justice Witness Intermediary Scheme and is referred to as a non-registered intermediary. (See O'Mahony (2010); O'Mahony, Smith, and Milne (2011) for a detailed explanation of the intermediary role).

Expert witness testimony at the original trial in *R v Cox* (2012) advised the court that the defendant was fit to plead. The trial judge had documented that in the absence of an intermediary, he himself would play 'part of the role which an intermediary, if available, would otherwise have played'. The Court of Appeal was informed that 'the absence of an intermediary played a part in the decision by the appellant not to give evidence, although it was not the only reason for not calling him to give evidence on his own behalf'. The Court of Appeal concluded that whilst it acknowledged the contribution of intermediaries in appropriate cases, it was not going so far as to conclude that whenever the process would be improved by the availability of an intermediary, it would be mandatory for an intermediary to be made available. Critically, the Court of Appeal noted that part of the trial judge's general responsibilities is to deal with specific communication problems faced by any defendant or indeed any witness.

The Criminal Practice Directions (2013; 3E) state 'The judiciary is responsible for controlling questioning. Over-rigorous or repetitive cross-examination of a child or vulnerable witness should be stopped. Intervention by the judge, magistrates or intermediary (if any) is minimised if questioning, taking account of the individual's communication needs, is discussed in advance and ground rules are agreed and adhered to'. The directions to the court are quite clear and whilst they are to be lauded, this paper raises the question of the ability of the judiciary and counsel to fully comprehend a vulnerable person's communication difficulties and intervene appropriately, if necessary, in the absence of an intermediary.

An example of a judge's intervention at trial with a vulnerable defendant, where an intermediary was present, has previously been documented (O'Mahony 2012). On that occasion the court transcript revealed the judge addressed the defendant who had a learning disability in the following terms:

> Hang on, let's keep a balance here. Miss (X), if you don't understand Mr (XX) questions, you say so. That is simple. If you don't say

that you don't understand we are entitled to assume that you do understand.

Communication professionals who work with adults with a learning disability will recognise instantly from the judge's statement above that the vocabulary and complexity of the language used is likely to be too advanced to be understood by a vulnerable person with a learning disability. Additionally, the judge does not appear to recognise the difficulties that a person with a learning disability may have both in recognising that they don't actually understand a question, and even if they do recognise a problem, informing a person in a position of power of such difficulties. We know that legal professionals may also have a different understanding of the term 'leading questions' to that of communication professionals and that opinions also may differ on the use of recommended question formats (Krahenbuhl 2011). We also know that there remain significant discrepancies amongst academics and practitioners over how best to categorise different question types (Oxburgh, Myklebust, and Grant 2010).

CASE STUDY: VULNERABILITY IDENTIFIED BUT NOT FULLY UNDERSTOOD BY THE COURT

The focus of the remainder of this paper is on a different trial transcript from a trial which took place in the Greater London area in the second half of 2014. Clearly, the Criminal Practice Directions (2013) were available at this time in addition to a wealth of 'toolkits' available from The Advocate's Gateway informing the legal profession about the questioning of vulnerable people at court. The author of this paper was an intermediary at this trial and present throughout the trial, but crucially, not for the individual who this transcript relates to, who will be referred to as Defendant 1 for the remainder of this paper.

It is evident from the transcript that Counsel for Defendant 1 advised the court at the commencement of examination-in-chief of the client:

> I only reiterate what I said to Your Honour very early in this trial; clearly he is a gentleman who does not require an intermediary but he does have difficulties which are (inaudible). I have obviously advised (Defendant 1) that he cannot speak to me during his evidence and if he does not understand something, he must not feel shy indicating to Your Honour, or whoever is asking the question.

The trial judge responded:

> Absolutely, I will make that quite clear to him. He can raise anything with me in court. I say anything; raise with me any queries about any

of the questions with me in court. We will obviously be continuing to have the half-hour breaks so that will assist him.

Counsel's comment above requires some unpacking as to the decision-making process that culminated in no intermediary assessment being requested. The court had been advised that Defendant 1 resided in supported housing with the co-defendant who incidentally had an intermediary (author of this paper) present throughout the trial. The court was aware that the vulnerabilities of Defendant 1 included possible learning difficulties. During the trial, prior to Defendant 1 giving evidence, the court was informed via the prison where Defendant 1 was on remand that concerns had been raised at the prison that he may be displaying traits of autism. So, it would seem that even when in possession of knowledge about these 'vulnerability risks' counsel formed the opinion that an intermediary assessment was not required.

The following excerpts are taken from the trial transcript of the cross-examination of Defendant 1. Prosecution Counsel's second question is documented below followed by the judge's intervention and a second attempt at the question by Prosecution Counsel. The asterisked words have been changed to provide anonymity.

> Counsel: Always been good friends. On the day of the incident, 'the *food** incident' we have heard that he was ushered out of the kitchen over a 'food' incident at *Naomi's**. Did you hear about that on that day? On the day it happened? Do you understand?
>
> Defendant 1: No
>
> Judge: Just break it down.
>
> Counsel: Sorry. When you went to *Naomi's** flat on the evening that you were arrested, do you remember you went to *Naomi's** flat on the evening you were arrested and this incident happened with the pushing?
>
> Defendant 1: Yes

Importantly, the judge intervened after counsel's first attempt at asking a question. However, it is unclear what relation the reworded question has to the initial attempt, and indeed the second attempt at constructing the question is not straightforward.

Shortly after responding to the above question counsel then asks three questions in one go:

All right, what was that about? What were the reasons you were there for? What did you wish to speak to him?

Whilst some of the questions in cross-examination were constructed in an easy to comprehend manner there were others that were not. Of concern is that there were no interventions by the judge to clarify some of these misunderstandings.

Counsel: You say that we should pay attention to that because that is the reason why he is presumably lying.

Defendant 1: Sorry, say that again, I'm lost.

Counsel: You were asked why is *N** saying all these things against you, yes?

Defendant 1: Yes

Counsel: One of the things you said was because he thought he might have been barred from the sheltered housing. Barred from coming to visit *Naomi**.

Defendant 1: Yes, yes.

Counsel: You gave us this a few moments ago.

Defendant 1: Yes.

It is possible that the defendant may be acquiescing or being compliant to the questions by answering 'yes' (Gudjonsson 2003; Ridley, Gabbert, and La Rooy 2013; Drake 2010). Acquiescence occurs when a vulnerable person answers a question in the affirmative as they think that this is the answer that the questioner is looking for. Compliance on the other hand is where a vulnerable person provides an account or an answer, as a means to getting away from the uncomfortable environment, for example the witness stand, even though they are aware that they are not providing an accurate answer. In essence, the vulnerable person feels pressured to respond. Meanwhile, further miscommunication is evident in the case study transcript but on this occasion the judge intervenes to try and resolve the issues. Regardless of these interventions it is not clear whether the defendant is acquiescing or whether he understands what he is being asked. We need to always carefully check out a sequence of 'yes' answers in case acquiescence is occurring.

Counsel: Do you remember the police officer said he saw some people running into the block?

Defendant 1: Running.

Counsel: From *Main** Street. Do you remember that evening that he gave today?

Defendant 1: No. No, say that again.

Judge: No, no, you are not being asked to remember something that you saw. You are being asked to remember something that was said today.

Counsel: Today

Judge: I think there is a distinction there we need to be quite careful about.

Counsel: Yes, sorry, Your Honour. One of the police officers stood in the witness box today and said when he and Mr *Smith**, PC *Smith** arrived, he looked down the road and could see three figures.

Judge: Three people.

Defendant 1: Yes

Counsel: Three people

Defendant 1: Yes

Counsel: Running into 23 *South** Street, the communal doors.

Defendant: Yes

Judge: Yes? That is what counsel is asking.

Defendant 1: All right, ok.

Judge: Do you remember that?

Defendant 1: Yes.

Judge: Good, right.

The dialogue above highlights issues including the use of highly complex abstract language which may be very difficult to deconstruct for someone with any level of learning disability and /or autistic traits ('Do you remember that evening that he gave today? Later in the cross-examination the Defendant is asked 'In your mind, you could answer those questions, could you not? You could say 'no, I did not do that?''). Counsel and the judge may not be aware that the defendant may be trying to comprehend the entire dialogue and that this may be fatiguing for the defendant.

If there is any doubt about the vulnerability of this defendant in terms of communication then the following dialogue would seem to illustrate such vulnerability. It also illustrates how difficult counsel appears to find articulating a question about the point he wishes to address.

Counsel: Did you know that you had the same solicitor in your interview that he had in his interview?

Defendant 1: That's impossible. Say that again?

Counsel: All right. He was interviewed, ok?

Defendant 1: Yes.

Counsel: He had the same solicitor in his interview that you had at the same time.

Judge: It is agreed that there was the same solicitor. The interviews took place at different times.

Defendant 1: Oh, yes. Yes.

Judge: The solicitor was at both of the interviews.

Towards the end of the cross-examination another example of miscommunication appears to take place and counsel asks a question that may make uncomfortable reading to anyone who works with vulnerable people.

Counsel: It was fresh in your mind, was it not? It was fresh in your mind, fresh in your memory?

Defendant 1: Fresh? Yes, yes.

Counsel: It was recent?

Defendant 1: Yes.

Counsel: It just happened the day before.

Defendant 1: Can you repeat that again?

Counsel: Sorry. It had happened the day before. You were sitting in the interview room the day after the incident, were you not?

Defendant 1: I...

Counsel: The police interview, the police lady asking you question.

Judge: You had the interview and it was the day after you had been arrested that you had the interview.

Defendant 1: Okay.

Counsel: Do you deliberately choose to be confused when it is a difficult question I am asking you?

Defendant 1: Sorry

Counsel: Do you deliberately choose to be confused before the jury when you are asked difficult questions?

Defendant 1: No. No, I don't.

Counsel: Because I suggest you do have the ability to speak at times and sometimes you do not.

Defendant 1: Yes.

Notably, the judge does not intervene at this point and neither does defence counsel object to the questioning.

THE NECESSITY FOR GROUND RULES HEARINGS

Ground Rules Hearings offer an excellent opportunity for all counsel in the case, the judge and the intermediary, if one has been allocated to the case, to have a detailed discussion about how to best communicate with the vulnerable witness or defendant (Plotnikoff and Woolfson 2015; *Ground Rules Hearing Checklist* 2015). Following the cross-examination of

Defendant 1 the author of this paper considered it essential that the court was made aware of the vulnerabilities of the second defendant and that a thorough Ground Rules Hearing took place prior to the commencement of the cross-examination. Ideally, counsel would consider the questions that he wished to raise ahead of cross-examination and share these, or at least some of these, with the intermediary prior to the cross-examination of Defendant 2. The judge made his opinion clear on this latter point:

> I am conscious of the fact though that counsel is quite experienced in this case...I think rather than me laying down any strict rules or asking for questions to be written out beforehand to be checked (by the intermediary), I do not think that is really practical. I would hope that we would be able to get through this; I mean obviously with the intermediary's intervention.

Later in the dialogue with the intermediary the judge makes the following statement:

> I think I can also, I hope, give you some reassurance that the court and the bar have experience of dealing with people with various difficulties and disabilities.

The courts are advancing in their knowledge of how to manage cases with vulnerable defendants and they are helped greatly by judgments from the higher courts. In *Lubemba* (2014) the Appeal Court stated

> So as to avoid any unfortunate misunderstanding at trial, it would be an entirely reasonable step for a judge at the ground rules hearing to invite defence advocates to reduce their questions to writing in advance.

In *Lubemba* (2014) the court also made it clear that the judge has a duty to intervene, therefore, if an advocate's questioning is confusing or inappropriate. The issue that needs to be addressed though is whether it is reasonable to expect the judge to have the knowledge and skills to highlight a miscommunication in all cases and the expertise to rephrase a question in a developmentally appropriate manner so that the vulnerable defendant is not further confused.

DISCUSSION

Earlier in this paper reference was made to the *R v Cox* (2012) case where the trial judge and counsel were tasked with adapting the trial process to enable a vulnerable defendant to comprehend the proceedings in the absence of an intermediary. The higher court later ruled that the trial judge 'conducted the proceedings with appropriate and necessary caution from start to finish and that the appellant's conviction followed a fair trial'. This finding may now be used to advise courts how to approach the trial of a vulnerable defendant if a suitably qualified intermediary cannot be located in England and Wales. Leaving aside the *Cox* case, this paper raises concerns that it may not always be the case that counsel and judges possess the skills to ask developmentally appropriate questions and to identify, intervene and most importantly rectify communication breakdown when it occurs between counsel and a vulnerable defendant (or witness). This paper has provided examples where the answer 'yes' given by the vulnerable defendant has been accepted by the court when indeed the affirmative answer may have been acquiescence on the part of the defendant and used to mask the defendant's confusion.

S104 of the Coroners and Justice Act (2009) has yet to be implemented in England and Wales and intermediaries are allocated seemingly on an ad hoc basis to vulnerable defendants. Whilst we await implementation of this scheme we have seen many courts use common law powers to allocate intermediaries to vulnerable defendant cases. The Northern Ireland Registered Intermediary pilot scheme has recently been evaluated (*Evaluation of the Northern Ireland Pilot Registered Intermediary Scheme* 2015). In Northern Ireland vulnerable suspects have access to a Registered Intermediary during police interview, unlike their counterparts in England and Wales (O'Mahony, Milne, and Grant 2012). Vulnerable defendants have access to an intermediary during oral testimony only, in Northern Ireland, rather than throughout the trial as used in common law in many cases in England and Wales. The evaluation of the Northern Ireland Scheme claims that the impartiality of the intermediary would be questioned if the intermediary were to be present with a defendant throughout the trial. There is no robust academic evidence to substantiate this claim in terms of how members of the jury might perceive the intermediary function and it is recommended that academic research is conducted before such conclusions are drawn. We are beginning to understand how intermediaries internalise their function when engaging in the intermediary role with vulnerable defendants but there is still a dearth of research in this area (O'Mahony et al 2016; O'Mahony 2013). It is also apparent from anecdotal evidence that the courts may be confused at times between the different functions of the intermediary and the expert witness in vulnerable defendant cases (Plotnikoff and Woolfson 2015).

It is evident that progress continues to be made in how the criminal courts strive to deliver equity of service to vulnerable defendants (Cooper and Wurtzel 2013) but concerns have been raised that we have not moved far enough (Hoyano 2010). The findings from the higher courts, as illustrated in

Lubemba (2014) are increasing the momentum to change practice but legal professionals must not become complacent and must realise that there is still some way to go in improving communication with vulnerable persons in the legal context. Intermediaries are one valuable resource that must be utilised when available.

Finally, advocates have a number of questions to reflect on. Does the current system encourage and enable advocates to regularly access trial transcripts and to examine a written record of their cross-examination skills? Do advocates value feedback from peers and indeed are they suitably skilled to both deliver such feedback constructively and to receive feedback without internalising it as criticism? How do advocates internalise feedback from professionals from outside the legal profession, for example intermediaries? Academia continues to develop an interest in this area and hopefully we will see more examples of excellent advocacy, whilst at the same time not shying away from examples of less skilled practice.

References:

The Advocacy Training Council. Excellence in Advocacy: Training the trainer. 2015 [cited 09.03.15]. Available from http://www.advocacytrainingcouncil.org/images/trainingthetrainersmanual2015.pdf.

Cooper, P, and D Wurtzel. 2013. "A day late and a dollar short: In search of an intermediary scheme for vulnerable defendants in England and Wales." *Criminal Law Review* no. 1:4-22.

Drake, K.E. 2010. "Interrogative suggestibility: Life adversity, neuroticism, and compliance." *Personality and Individual Differences* no. 48:493-498.

Evaluation of the Northern Ireland Pilot Registered Intermediary Scheme. 2015. Available from http://www.dojni.gov.uk/index/publications/publication-categories/pubs-criminal-justice/ri-post-project-reviewfeb15.pdf

Ground Rules Hearing Checklist. 2015 [cited 09.03.15]. Available from http://www.theadvocatesgateway.org/images/toolkits/groundruleshearingchecklist06032015.pdf.

Gudjonsson, G.H. 2003. *The Psychology of Interrogations and Confessions: A Handbook.* Chichester: John Wiley & Sons Ltd.

Hoyano, L.C.H. 2010. "Coroners and Justice Act 2009: special measures directions take two: entrenching unequal access to justice?" *Criminal Law Review*:345-367.

Intermediaries: Step by Step. 2015 [cited 09.03.15. Available from http://www.theadvocatesgateway.org/images/toolkits/16intermediaries stepbystep060315.pdf.

Keane, A. 2012. "Cross-examination of vulnerable witnesses - towards a blueprint for re-professionalisation." *The International Journal of Evidence and Proof* no. 16:175-198.

Kebbell, M.R., C. Hatton, and S.D. Johnson. 2004. "Witnesses with intellectual disabilities in court: What questions are asked and what influence do they have?" *Legal and Criminological Psychology* no. 9:23-35.

Krahenbuhl, S.J. 2011. "Effective and Appropriate Communication with Children in Legal Proceedings According to Lawyers and Intermediaries." *Child Abuse Review* no. 20 (6):407-420.

O'Mahony, B.M. 2010. "The emerging role of the Registered Intermediary with the vulnerable witness and offender: facilitating communication with the police and members of the judiciary." *British Journal of Learning Disabilities* no. 38:232-237.

O'Mahony, B.M. 2012. "Accused of murder: supporting the communication needs of a vulnerable defendant at court and at the police station." *Journal of Learning Disabilities and Offending Behaviour.* no. 3 (2):77-84.

O'Mahony, B.M. 2013. *How do intermediaries experience their role in facilitating communication for vulnerable defendants?*, DCrimJ thesis Institute of Criminal Justice Studies, University of Portsmouth, Portsmouth.

O'Mahony, B.M., J. Creaton, K. Smith, and R. Milne. 2016 "Developing a professional identity in a new work environment: the views of defendant intermediaries working in the criminal courts." *Journal of Forensic Practice* Volume 18, Issue 2: 155-166.

O'Mahony, B.M., R. Milne, and T. Grant. 2012. "To Challenge, or not to Challenge? Best practice when interviewing vulnerable suspects." *Policing: A Journal of Policy and Practice* no. 6 (3):301-313.

O'Mahony, B.M., K. Smith, and R. Milne. 2011. "The early identification of vulnerable witnesses prior to an investigative interview." *British Journal of Forensic Practice* no. 13 (2):114-123.

Oxburgh, G.E., T. Myklebust, and T. Grant. 2010. "The question of question types in police interviews: a review of the literature from a psychological and linguistic perspective." *The International Journal of Speech, Language and the Law* no. 17 (1):45-66.

Plotnikoff, J, and R Woolfson. 2015. *Intermediaries in the criminal justice system*. Great Britain: Policy Press.

Ridley, A.M., F. Gabbert, and D.J. La Rooy. 2013. *Suggestibility in Legal Contexts*. Chichester, England: Wiley-Blackwell.

Criminal Cases

Criminal Practice Directions [2013] EWCA Crim 1631

R v Cox [2012] EWCA Crim 549

R v Lubemba [2014] EWCA Crim 2064

Valuable Lessons and Poor Relations: Comparing the English Criminal and Family Justice Systems' Approaches to Vulnerable and Intimidated Witnesses

PROFESSOR PENNY COOPER[1]

INTRODUCTION

The Advocate's Gateway[2] held its inaugural international conference, *Addressing Vulnerability in Justice System*, in London on 20th June 2015. In a session entitled 'Poor Relations?'[3] Sir James Munby, President of the Family Division of England and Wales, opined that family law was lagging "woefully behind criminal law" in terms of procedures for the inclusion of children and vulnerable adults. Children are currently "invisible" in family proceedings he remarked[4], and in many public law cases parents have

---

[1] Co-founder and Chair of The Advocate's Gateway, visiting professor, City University London and senior research fellow at the Institute of Criminal Policy Research (University of London), barrister and academic associate 39 Essex Chambers, London. The author was also a member of the Vulnerable Witnesses and Children Working Group. The author has designed and delivered the registered intermediary training for England and Wales, Northern Ireland and Australia since the inception of the schemes in each jurisdiction.
[2] Theadvocatesgateway.org is a website with free advocacy guidance and training resources. It is hosted and funded by The Advocacy Training Council.
[3] Sir James Munby at *Addressing Vulnerability in Justice Systems*, The Advocate's Gateway Conference, held by The Advocacy Training Council (ATC) at The Law Society, Chancery Lane, London, June 19-20, 2015
[4] In the family courts it is very rare for a child to be present in person though, when they can be ascertained, their 'wishes and feelings' must be taken into account - see section 1 (3) (a) of the Children Act 1989.

learning difficulties.[5] He noted that procedures for taking evidence from victims are inadequate for example in family cases a perpetrator might cross-examine the complainant, something which legislation prevents in the criminal court[6] and Mr Justice Wood, had drawn attention to this as long ago as 2006.[7]

This was not the first time the President had talked about the need for a sea-change in the family court's approach. Almost exactly a year earlier, in June 2014 the President drew attention to the issues in his *'12th View from the President's Chambers'*.[8] He asked two high court judges, Mr Justice Hayden and Ms Justice Russell, to chair a Vulnerable Witnesses and Children Working Group. The working group ('WG') produced its final report[9] in March 2015 and included recommendations for new court rules and practice directions:

> The purpose is to give prominence and emphasis to the treatment of children and parties in family proceedings; to emphasise the importance of the role of the child and the need to identify the necessary support /special measures for vulnerable witnesses and/ or parties from the outset of any proceedings, or at the earliest opportunity.[10]

The definition of 'vulnerable', the use of ground rules hearings, the use of witness intermediaries, pre-recording of cross-examination, and specialist training of advocates were all mentioned in the WG report and are all existing features in the criminal justice system. What lessons are there for the family justice system as it attempts to ride the coat tails of the criminal justice system?

THE DEFINITION OF 'VULNERABLE'

The WG concluded:

> The term vulnerable and intimidated witness should remain in use as it is not desirable for the family court procedure to become distanced or uncoupled from the practice and procedure as it has developed in the criminal justice system. The term should be to be extended to cover the parties as well as witnesses.[11]

---

[5] The exact figures are not known.
[6] Ss. 34 – 40, The Youth Justice and Criminal Evidence Act 1999.
[7] *H v L and R* [2006] EWHC 3099 (Fam), [2007] 2 FLR 162.
[8] Sir James Munby, (2014) Fam Law 978.
[9] Vulnerable Witnesses and Children Working Group, "Report of the Vulnerable Witnesses & Children Working Group" (London: Judiciary of England and Wales, 2015).
[10] Ibid.
[11] Vulnerable Witnesses and Children Working Group, "Report of the Vulnerable

The concept of the 'vulnerable witness' took root in the report *Speaking up for Justice*[12] which in turn led to the Youth Justice and Criminal Evidence Act 1999.'[13] Rather than simply use the umbrella term 'vulnerable' for those are at risk of unfair treatment if adjustments are not made, the Youth Justice and Criminal Evidence Act 1999 (YJCEA 1999) divides them into two groups, the 'vulnerable' and the 'intimidated'.[14]

The tests for eligibility as a vulnerable or intimidated witness are different as is the range of special measures that are available to them. There are in total eight 'special measures' in the YJCEA 1999: S23 Screening witness from accused; s24 Evidence by live link; s25 Evidence given in private; s26 Removal of wigs and gowns; s27 Video recorded evidence in chief; s28 Video recorded cross-examination or re-examination; s29 Examination of witness through intermediary; s30 Aids to communication. In addition since June 2011 there has been a provision for a witness 'supporter' to be permitted in the live link room with a vulnerable witness.[15] Section 28 thus far has been implemented as a pilot scheme only at three Crown Courts.[16]

If a witness is eligible for special measures an application may be made to the judge or the court may make a special measures direction of its own motion.[17] Eligibility for these special measures is defined in sections 16 and 17 of the YJCEA 1999. Section 16 applies to those who are eligible for assistance on the 'grounds of age or incapacity'. All children (i.e. those under 18) are eligible as are those for whom the quality of their evidence is likely to be diminished due to a mental disorder, a significant impairment of social functioning or a physical disability or disorder. Intermediaries and communications aids are only available to witness who are vulnerable on the grounds of age or incapacity i.e. section 16 'vulnerable' witnesses not section 17 'intimidated' witnesses.

Section 17 applies to those for whom the quality of their evidence is likely to be diminished through 'fear or distress'; special measures in

---

Witnesses & Children Working Group" (London: Judiciary of England and Wales, 2015) 22

[12] Home Office, "Speaking up for Justice: Report of the Interdepartmental Working Group on the Treatment of Vulnerable or Intimidated Witnesses in the Criminal Justice System" (London: Home Office,1998).

[13] Penny Cooper and David Wurtzel, "Better the second time around? Department of Justice Registered Intermediaries Schemes and lessons from England and Wales", *Northern Ireland Legal Quarterly* 65 (2014): 1.

[14] Chapter 1 of the Youth Justice and Criminal Evidence Act 1999 (YJCEA 1999) is titled 'Special measures directions in case of vulnerable and intimidated witnesses'.

[15] This was implemented on 27th June 2011. Section 102 of the Coroners and Justice Act 2009 amends section 24 so that the court can direct a person specified by the court (a witness supporter) can accompany the witness in the live link room.

[16] Special measures were not introduced all at the same time. The intermediary (section 29) started as a pilot in 2003 and was rolled out nationally by 2008. The last to be introduced is pre-recorded cross-examination; a pilot scheme began at the very end of 2013.

[17] Section 19 (1) of the YJCEA 1999.

section 23 to 28 are potentially available to the witness. In 2011 section 17 was amended[18] so that eligibility is automatically extended to witnesses in specified gun and knife crime offences. There is also special provision for sexual offences complainants so that their video-recorded statement may be automatically admissible unless this would not be in the interests of justice or would not maximise the quality of the complainant's evidence.[19]

When Parliament passed the YJCEA 1999 the accused was specifically excluded from eligibility for special measures.[20] However amendments[21] now allow the court to direct that, in appropriate circumstances, the defendant gives evidence by live link and also may be accompanied while giving evidence. A legislative provision introducing the intermediary for the vulnerable accused has not yet been brought into force and, if it were, the statutory test for a defendant's eligibility for an intermediary would be different to that for a witness.[22]

GROUND RULES HEARINGS

The Working Group acknowledged the significance of ground rules hearings, a new development in criminal cases involving vulnerable witnesses:

> The ground rules hearings currently being written into the Criminal Procedure Rules (due to come into force in April 2015) should prove useful in drafting the PD.[23]

Ground rules hearings in criminal cases[24] started off as a concept in the author's classroom then, on a case by case basis, intermediaries for vulnerable witnesses sought and obtained a discussion with the trial judge and the advocates prior to the cross-examination. The author's 2009 survey of intermediaries[25] revealed that ground rules hearings occurred in fewer than half the intermediary cases in the study. Two years later the

---

[18] Section 99 of the Coroners and Justice Act 2009.
[19] Section 101 of the Coroners and Justice Act 2009 inserts this as a new section 22A of the YJCEA.
[20] Section 16 (1), the Youth Justice and Criminal Evidence Act 1999.
[21] 33A and 33BA of the YJCEA 1999.
[22] Section 104 of the Coroners and Justice Act 2009.
[23] Vulnerable Witnesses and Children Working Group, "Report of the Vulnerable Witnesses & Children Working Group" (London: Judiciary of England and Wales, 2015) 19.
[24] Penny Cooper, Paula Backen and Ruth Marchant, "Getting to Grips with Ground Rules Hearings: A Checklist for Judges, Advocates and Intermediaries to Promote Fair Treatment of Vulnerable People in Court" , *Crim. L.R.* (2015) 6, 420 – 435.
[25] Penny Cooper, "Tell Me What's Happening 2009", (London: City University, 2010) 4. http://www.city.ac.uk/__data/assets/pdf_file/0008/92519/Tell_Me_What27s_Happening_-_Registered_Intermediary_Survey_20.pdf (accessed August 23, 2015)

Criminal Practice Directions[26] included that a ground rules hearing should occur in cases with vulnerable witnesses and defendants even if there is no intermediary.

In October 2014 in the case of *Lubemba*[27] the Court of Appeal Criminal Division underlined that it is the judge's duty to control questioning and if a witness is vulnerable there should be a ground rules hearing, 'save in very exceptional circumstances'.[28] In January 2015 Sir Brian Leveson, President of the Queen's Bench Division, endorsed 'the ground rules approach', suggesting it might be used for expert evidence too.[29] On 6 April 2015, based on the author's results of a further survey of intermediaries[30], the Criminal Procedure Rules (CPR) were amended to include ground rules hearings.

At CPR 3.9.7 under 'Case preparation and progression' it states:

'(7) Where directions for appropriate treatment and questioning are required, the court must-

(a) invite representations by the parties and by any intermediary; and

(b) set ground rules for the conduct of the questioning, which rules may include—

(i) a direction relieving a party of any duty to put that party's case to a witness or a defendant in its entirety,

(ii) directions about the manner of questioning,

(iii) directions about the duration of questioning,

(iv) if necessary, directions about the questions that may or may not be asked,

(v) where there is more than one defendant, the allocation among them of the topics about which a witness may be asked, and

---

[26] [2013] EWCA Crim 1631 at 3E.
[27] [2014] EWCA Crim 2064.
[28] Ibid at para 44.
[29] Lord Justice Leveson, "Review of Efficiency in Criminal Proceedings" (London: Judiciary of England and Wales, 2015) 8.3.1.
[30] Penny Cooper , "Highs and Lows: The 4th Intermediary Survey (2014)" (London: Kingston University 2014). http://www.city.ac.uk/__data/assets/pdf_file/0011/280496/INTERMEDIARY-SURVEY-REPORT-5-July-2015.pdf (accessed August 23, 2015)

(vi) directions about the use of models, plans, body maps or similar aids to help communicate a question or an answer.

Judges use ground rules hearings to set the parameters for the fair treatment of vulnerable witnesses, and vulnerable defendants too.[31] The approach has been adopted in family courts[32], for example:

> The mother gave evidence via live video-link, and with the assistance of Ms Fletcher, the intermediary. This followed not just a general 'ground rules' hearing before the commencement of the hearing, but a further, specific ground rules hearing to consider the issues which would arise during her evidence. All counsel were alerted to the need to keep the questions short and simple, to allow time for consideration, not to use abstracts or tag-questions.[33]

USE OF INTERMEDIARIES

The WG said,

> It is difficult to understand any argument that would suggest that intermediaries (like translators or interpreters) should not be present when necessary for the purposes of meeting with professionals, particularly legal representatives out of court and during the preparation of the vulnerable party's case. The position of funding, which is dealt with on an ad hoc basis, is unsatisfactory. If access to justice for vulnerable parties is not to be denied it is a matter which requires urgent review and clarification.[34]

Section 29 of the YJCEA 1999 defines the role of the intermediary in the criminal courts:

The function of an intermediary is to communicate —

(a) to the witness, questions put to the witness, and

---

[31] Penny Cooper, Paula Backen and Ruth Marchant, "Getting to Grips with Ground Rules Hearings: A Checklist for Judges, Advocates and Intermediaries to Promote Fair Treatment of Vulnerable People in Court", *Crim. L.R.* (2015) 6, 420 – 435.
[32] *Re A (A Child) (Vulnerable Witness: Fact Finding)* [2013] EWHC 2124 (Fam) appears to be the earliest reported mention of a family judge holding a ground rules hearing.
[33] Mr Justice Cobb in *Newcastle City Council v WM & Ors* [2015] EWFC 42 at para 29.
[34] Vulnerable Witnesses and Children Working Group, "Report of the Vulnerable Witnesses & Children Working Group" (London: Judiciary of England and Wales, 2015) 13.

(b) to any person asking such questions, the answers given by the witness in reply to them, and to explain such questions or answers so far as necessary to enable them to be understood by the witness or person in question.[35]

Practise developed such that the role is now much broader than first envisaged and this is reflected in a detailed intermediary procedural guidance manual for the criminal justice system.[36]

The police and Crown Prosecution Service request the services of an intermediary for a witness via the National Crime Agency.[37] The intermediary will assess the witness, advise the police officer how best to communicate with the witness, write a report for the advocates and judge, attend a witness familiarisation visit, attend the ground rules hearing to discuss with the judge and advocates how to achieve best evidence for this witness, monitor communication in court (usually sitting alongside the witness) and intervene during cross-examination if the question has not been put in a way that the witness can deal with. The role has delivered 'fresh insights' into the criminal justice system.[38]

Soon after the introduction of intermediaries in criminal cases, it became clear that there would be a need for them in family cases[39] but there remains an absence of legislation or even guidance about how they should operate in family cases. Nevertheless there are several family court judgments referring to intermediary involvement. For example,

Intermediary involvement

5. Having identified some of the failures in the case, I turn next, and briefly, to one of its significant redeeming features. The role of the intermediary service.

6. I wish to pay particular tribute to Clare Jones and Rebecca Fletcher from Communicourt Limited who offered an excellent intermediary service to the Court for the mother in this case. The mother has significant communication difficulties, both with understanding and using language; this is likely to be attributable

---

[35] Section 29 (2) the Youth Justice and Criminal Evidence Act 1999.
[36] Penny Cooper and David Wurtzel, *Registered Intermediary Procedural Guidance Manual*, (London: Ministry of Justice 2015) (new edition in print).
[37] Penny Cooper, *Intermediaries Step by Step Toolkit 16* March 2015 (London: ATC 2015) at theadvocatesgateway.org/ toolkits (accessed August 23, 2015).
[38] The Rt. Hon. The Lord Judge, Lord Chief Justice of England and Wales, 7 September 2011, at the 17th Australian Institute of Judicial Administration Conference in 'Vulnerable Witnesses in the Administration of Criminal Justice'.
[39] Penny Cooper, "Child witnesses in family proceedings: should intermediaries be showing us the way?" Family Law, (2011) 41, pp. 397-403.

in part to her learning disability, and in part to acquiring English as a second language.

7. Ms Jones' report, dated 20 February 2015, was clear and practical, providing guidance about how best to manage the case in a way which would optimise the mother's participation. Ms Jones was regrettably unable to attend the final hearing, and the intermediary service was therefore provided by Ms Fletcher, who performed her role with great skill and discretion. Ground rules had been set by HHJ Hudson at the IRH; these were re-visited at the outset of the hearing. Specific ground rules were set for the mother's evidence, which we all endeavoured conscientiously to observe.

8. Overall, I was satisfied that the mother had been enabled to participate in the process as fully and effectively as could possibly be achieved. I am indebted to the intermediary service for its assistance.[40]

PRE-RECORDING OF CROSS-EXAMINATION

The WG recommended arrangements which would include 'pre-recording of evidence currently being piloted in 3 Crown Courts'.[41]

The criminal justice legislation is contained in section 28 of the YJCEA 1999:

Video recorded cross-examination or re-examination.

(1) Where a special measures direction provides for a video recording to be admitted under section 27 as evidence in chief of the witness, the direction may also provide—

(a) for any cross-examination of the witness, and any re-examination, to be recorded by means of a video recording; and

(b) for such a recording to be admitted, so far as it relates to any such cross-examination or re-examination, as evidence of the witness under cross-examination or on re-examination, as the case may be.

Under this provision, not only can the witness's police video-recorded interview be used in place of a witness's 'live' evidence in chief, cross-

---

[40] Cobb J in *Newcastle City Council v WM & Ors* [2015] EWFC 42.
[41] Vulnerable Witnesses and Children Working Group, "Report of the Vulnerable Witnesses & Children Working Group" (London: Judiciary of England and Wales, 2015) 19

examination and the re-examination may also be recorded. The idea of pre-recording is by no means a new one. In 1989 'The Pigot Report'[42] suggested pre-recording of child witness evidence:

> ...outside the courtroom in informal surroundings and ... video recorded. Nobody should be present in the same room as the child except the judge, advocates and a parent or supporter, but the accused should be able to hear and view the proceedings through closed circuit television or a two way mirror an communicate with his legal representatives.[43]

Of all the special measures in the criminal justice system, pre-recording of cross-examination and re-examination, or 'section 28'[44] as it is known for short, was the last one to be brought into effect. The implementation of section 28 was given fresh impetus in June 2013 following the publication of the *Home Affairs Committee (Second Report) Child sexual exploitation and the response to localised grooming.*[45] The day after publication of that report, a pilot scheme for pre-recorded cross-examination was announced by the Justice Secretary.[46] The venue for pre-recording is perhaps not exactly 'outside the courtroom in informal surroundings' as *The Pigot Report* envisaged; in the pilot scheme it takes place at the Crown Court in a designated live-link room set up with purpose-specific recording equipment.

Cross-examination and re-examination (if any) may be conducted by the advocates from the courtroom over the live link television screens, however in Leeds Crown Court it is more usual to find that the cross-examining advocate and the judge are in the live link room for the questioning.[47] NatCen Social Research conducted a series of interviews with professionals and witnesses in order to evaluate the pilot. A report will be sent to Ministers and 'made available later in the year'.[48]

Pre-recording of vulnerable witness evidence for the family court occurs on an ad hoc basis. In 2014 the author visited the Leeds family court

---

[42] Judge Thomas Pigot, Q.C., *Report of the Advisory Group on Video Evidence*, (London: Home Office, 1989). This report became known as 'the Pigot report'.
[43] Judge Thomas Pigot, Q.C., *Report of the Advisory Group on Video Evidence*, (London: Home Office, 1989), Summary of Recommendations, paragraph 4.
[44] Youth Justice and Criminal Evidence Act 1999.
[45] House of Commons Home Affairs Committee, Child sexual exploitation and the response to localised grooming, Second Report of 2013-2014, (London: House of Commons 2013), Recommendation 23. http://www.publications.parliament.uk/pa/cm201314/cmselect/cmhaff/68/6808.htm (August 20, 2015).
[46] Ministry of Justice, 11th June 2013, 'The most vulnerable victims are to be protected from the trauma of appearing in court, Justice Secretary Chris Grayling announced today.' https://www.gov.uk/government/news/victims-to-be-spared-from-harrowing-court-cases (accessed August 20, 2015).
[47] HHJ Cahill conversation with the author, June 2015.
[48] Baljit Wirk (Witness Policy, MoJ) email to the author August 14, 2015

and HHJ Heaton shared examples[49] of cases where testimony had been pre-recorded.

A parent in care proceedings with mental health difficulties gave evidence in a pre-recorded examination conducted by counsel in her chambers. All advocates and the judge contributed to the planning of topics to be covered and an intermediary helped counsel plan her questions. The recording of the witness's evidence was conducted by a professional third party who signed a confidentiality agreement. Questioning, including breaks, took three and half hours and an edited DVD lasting ninety minutes was admitted as evidence in the family proceedings.

An 8 year old child who was alleged to have been sexually abused by a family friend, had already given an ABE interview to the police, and was subsequently interviewed by an expert child psychiatrist in the family proceedings. All parties contributed to the planning of the psychiatrist's interview. The interview was recorded in a vulnerable witness interview suite at a local police station and the DVD recording used as evidence in the family proceedings. An order was subsequently made for the interview to be disclosed to the police so that it could be use it as evidence in related criminal proceedings.

TRAINING ADVOCATES

The WG recommends training of judges[50] and advocates the latter of which is being considered and developed by a group led by family high court judge Mr Justice Newton.[51] For decades academics and other observers have been bemoaning the lack of specialist training for criminal advocates who cross-examine children. In 2011 the observations came from within the profession when The Advocacy Training Council (ATC), in its Raising the Bar report[52], noted a pressing need for training for those working with

---

[49] These examples and others can been found in Toolkit 13 – Vulnerable Witnesses and Parties in the Family Courts - on The Advocate's Gateway http://www.theadvocatesgateway.org/images/toolkits/13vulnerablewitnessesandpartiesinthefamilycourts081114.pdf (accessed August 23, 2015)

[50] Vulnerable Witnesses and Children Working Group, "Report of the Vulnerable Witnesses & Children Working Group" (London: Judiciary of England and Wales, 2015), recommendation xii at page 26.

[51] Vulnerable Witnesses and Children Working Group, "Report of the Vulnerable Witnesses & Children Working Group" (London: Judiciary of England and Wales, 2015), recommendation xx at page 27.

[52] Advocacy Training Council, *Raising the Bar* (London: ATC, 2011). http://advocacytraining

vulnerable witnesses and defendants.[53]   After Raising the Bar the ATC took action and set up its own committee to take forward training plans for criminal advocates.

HHJ Rook chairs that committee ('The Rook Committee') which is overseeing the design of a course aimed at being both effective and affordable for criminal advocates. There is a tension between those two aims; it is widely accepted that effective advocacy training should be interactive and participative however there is virtually no budget available to develop this training for thousands of criminal advocates.

The Rook committee is formed of volunteers and also has the support and good will of justice system professionals including academics and intermediaries who assist with the development of the training. At the time of writing, ATC training materials (case studies and a filmed demonstration of best practice at a ground rules hearing) are still at the design stage. The ground rules approach will be a central feature of vulnerable witness advocacy training programme for all criminal advocates.[54]

CONCLUSIONS

The family and criminal justice systems' approach to enabling the effective participation of 'vulnerable' witnesses are theoretically aligned though practically still some distance a part. If implemented, the recommendations of the WG for new family court rules, practice directions and training will bring the two systems closer together. Those rules and practice directions should reflect lessons from the criminal justice system.

It could be argued that the term 'vulnerable' should be avoided by the family justice system: 'The paradox of employing the frame of 'vulnerability' is that it makes people more vulnerable. It does so by contributing to prejudices about disabled people' though there is there is no obvious term to replace it. [55] The WG expressed the desire that the family justice system should fall in line with criminal justice system terminology. However the family justice system could avoid the bifurcation of categories and simply refer to those who are at risk of unfair treatment as 'vulnerable', an umbrella term, rather develop separate rules 'vulnerable' or 'intimated' witnesses.

The family justice system should aim for a more straightforward eligibility test. The eligibility test for special measures has become complex

council.org/images/word/raisingthebar.pdf (accessed 23 August 2015)
[53] Penny Cooper , "Ticketing Talk Gets Serious" (London: LexisNexis Butterworth 2014) *Counsel*, November,12- 13.
[54] Angela Rafferty QC email to author, August 17, 2015
[55] Madeleine L'Engle, "It's high time we abandoned the language of vulnerability" (2015) https://makingrightsmakesense.wordpress.com/2015/08/05/its-high-time-we-abandoned-the-language-of-vulnerability-2/ (accessed August 18, 2015)

in the criminal justice system. Some criminal judges have commented that[56] they would prefer a simple test based on the 'interests of justice'. Such a test would more straightforward to apply albeit it could be argued such a test is too simple and would lack certainty as to eligibility. A form of wording would need to be identified that strikes the right balance.

The widespread and effective use of ground rules hearings in the family justice system is only likely to be achieved if there are specific family court rules and practice directions. In the absence of family court rules, it is more likely that practice will develop slowly (if at all) and inconsistently (as it did in the criminal courts). Rules would need to reflect the needs of the family court. For example *Newcastle City Council v WM & Ors*[57] demonstrates that when a party is vulnerable there is a need for not only one but two ground rules hearings; one at the start of the case to ensure the proceedings the vulnerable party's effective participation and another to set the parameters for their questioning if they choose to give evidence.

Whilst individual cases provide examples of intermediaries operating in family justice, overall the situation is far from satisfactory. Unlike the criminal justice system, the family justice system has no 'Registered Intermediary' scheme where the intermediaries are trained, accredited, matched with witnesses and quality assured. There is no definition of the role, no procedural guidance, no clarity over who pays, no quality assurance etc in the family justice system. Without the intervention of the Ministry of Justice and significant expenditure to widen the intermediary scheme, it is hard to see how the family justice system will ever be more than an extremely poor relation in this regard.

Charles Geekie QC[58] expressed his embarrassment that the family court has section 96 of the Children Act 1989 which accommodates provision for all types of recorded evidence to be received, yet has never fully made use of it. Until a Supreme Court decision in 2010, there was a presumption that children ought not to give evidence in family proceedings.[59] In contrast, that the same year the Court of Appeal Criminal Division heard the case about a 4 year old girl who gave evidence at the Old Bailey. In that case the then Lord Chief Justice spelled out that the test of competence is no different for a child than it is for an adult witness.[60] Very young children can and do give evidence in criminal cases[61] but this remains practically unheard of in the family justice system.

---

[56] Crown Court judges in conversations with the author in 2015.
[57] [2015] EWFC 42.
[58] Speaking at The Advocate's Gateway conference on 20th June 2015.
[59] *Re W* [2010] UKSC 12.
[60] Section 53, Youth Justice and Criminal Evidence Act 1999.
[61] Ruth Marchant, "How Young Is Too Young?" *Child Abuse Review* (2013) DOI: 10.1002/car.2273.

If the criminal court pre-recording pilot evaluation is positive, the family court could consider pre-recording evidence of all witnesses, not just those who are children or otherwise vulnerable or intimidated. Arguably all witnesses in family cases, due to their circumstances are 'vulnerable' to some extent.[62] It could be done away from court and in informal surroundings. Potential advantages of pre-recorded evidence include reduced delay and distress for the witnesses, better recollection if questioning is closer to the time of the alleged event/s and reduced court hearing times.

The implementation of vulnerable witness advocacy training is taking years in the criminal justice system. It is likely to take a similar length of time in the family justice system if the development framework (i.e. judge-led committee of volunteers) is similar. The training being looked at is for qualified advocates. It is beginning to be recognised that cross-examination lessons taught to advocates 'go out of the window' for vulnerable witnesses.[63] It is surely time to review traditional pre and post-qualification teaching of cross-examination[64] so that it does not create bad habits which have to be unlearnt in vulnerable witness advocacy training.

The family justice is a poor relation to the criminal justice system but is aiming to improve through a series of court rules, practice directions and training. The ATC's 'Raising the Bar' report of 2011 coincided with a culture shift within the criminal justice system. The WG report may be coinciding with a similar culture shift in the family justice system. In 2015 an experienced family barrister, Gillian Geddes, powerfully described a case where she represented a vulnerable mother in family court case and complex adjustments were made.[65] The case, not just the outcome, had a profound effect on the mother. The case also led Geddes to question generally how cases are heard in the family court.

Perhaps the biggest lesson for the family justice system is that when so many parts require radical adjustment in order to make the system fair for those that it serves, it is time to consider redesigning the whole.

---

[62] Penny Cooper, "Speaking when they are spoken to: hearing vulnerable witnesses in care proceedings" *Child and Family Law Quarterly* (2014) 26(2), 132-151.
[63] Iain Morley, *The Devil's Advocate* (London: Sweet & Maxwell, 2015) 307
[64] These are exemplified by 'Irving Younger's 10 Commandments Of Cross Examination at UC Hastings College Of The Law' on YouTube at https://m.youtube.com/watch?v=dBP2if0l-a8 (accessed August 20, 2015).
[65] Gillian Geddes, "Safeguarding measures, intermediaries and vulnerable witnesses: footnotes from the trenches", *Family Law* (2015) 903.

Poor Relations?
Vulnerable in the Family Courts

CHARLES GEEKIE QC

The child was called as a witness, but said nothing. The court deprecates the calling of a child of this age as a witness. Although the learned judge had the court cleared as far as it can be cleared, is seems to us to be unfortunate that she was called and, with all respect to the learned judge, I am surprised that he allowed her to be called. The jury cannot attach any value to the evidence of a child of five; it is ridiculous to suppose that they could...in any circumstances to call a little child of the age of five seems to us to be most undesirable, and I hope it will not occur again.

R v Wallwork (1958) 42 Cr. App. R 153, Lord Goddard, Lord Chief Justice, 2nd April 1958.

INTRODUCTION

This paper will consider the arrangements in the family courts in England and Wales for the presentation and testing of the evidence of children and the vulnerable. The paper will set out the development of arrangements since the implementation of the Children Act 1989 and the arrangements as they are at present. It will then go on to look at the deficits in those arrangements and the proposals for change. It will argue that, despite a bright beginning (in 1989) the arrangements in the family courts have fallen behind those that apply in the criminal courts. The paper will conclude with a summary of the steps now being taken to rectify these deficits.

The quotation above, striking as it is to the modern eye, is produced to show that, indeed, much ground has been travelled since 1958.

THE CHILDREN ACT 1989

The title of this session asks the question: "Poor relations?" Are the family courts now the poor relations to the criminal courts in the way in which the vulnerable and the young are treated as witnesses? If this is so, it certainly was not intended to be so by policy makers and legislators in 1989.

The Children Act 1989 received Royal Assent just as the Pigot Committee[1] was considering the use of video recorded evidence of children in criminal proceedings. The prospect of such evidence left its mark (now perhaps rather faded) upon the Children Act, section 96 of which provides:

Evidence given by, or with respect to, children

(1) Subsection (2) applies in any civil proceedings where a child who is called as a witness in any civil proceedings does not, in the opinion of the court, understand the nature of an oath.

(2) The child's evidence may be heard by the court if, in its opinion –

    (a) he understands that it is his duty to speak the truth; and

    (b) he has sufficient understanding to justify his evidence being heard.

(3) The Lord Chancellor may, with the concurrence of the Lord Chief Justice, by order make provision for the admissibility of evidence which would otherwise be inadmissible under any rule of law relating to hearsay.

(4) An order under subsection (3) may only be made with respect to –

    (a) civil proceedings in general or such civil proceedings, or class of civil proceedings, as may be prescribed; and

    (b) evidence in connection with the upbringing, maintenance or welfare of a child.

(5) An order under subsection (3) –

---

[1] The Report of the Advisory Group on Video Evidence (Home Office December 1989).

(a) may, in particular, provide for the admissibility of statements which are made orally or in a prescribed form or which are recorded by any prescribed method of recording;

(b)may make different provision for different purposes and in relation to different descriptions of court; and

(c) may make such amendments and repeals in any enactment relating to evidence (other than in this Act) as the Lord Chancellor considers necessary or expedient in consequence of the provision made by the order.

Section 96(3) was introduced in order to reverse case law[2] that had established that whilst hearsay evidence was admissible in Wardship cases, it was not admissible in children's cases generally. The subsection led to what is now the *Children (Admissibility of Hearsay Evidence) Order 1993* (SI 1993/621):

In (b)(i) family proceedings...evidence given in connection with the upbringing, maintenance or welfare of a child shall be admissible notwithstanding any rule of law relating to hearsay.

At the time, this provision represented a significant departure from criminal proceedings, allowing for a far more flexible approach to be taken to the receipt of evidence concerning children. The provision has been much used in admitting documentary hearsay evidence about children. However, as will be seen, the opportunity to be more flexible in relation to the actual testimony of children was not taken up.

Section 96(5) was an important partner provision to subsection 3. The wording of subsection 5 is striking. It provides for statements to be admitted into evidence whether made "orally or in a prescribed form or which are recorded by any prescribed method of recording". In the context of the Pigot Committee's research it seems clear that, in 1989, the use of video recorded statements from children was in contemplation. No statutory instruments have been made pursuant to s96(5). There was an open door, in statute, to make provision for the receipt of children's testimony in a more flexible fashion. The 26 years since 1989 have seen no practical or realistic steps being taken towards the fulfilment of this ambition.

---

[2] *Re H (A Minor); Re K (Minors)(Child Abuse: Evidence)* [1989] 2 FLR 313.

CURRENT PRACTICE IN THE FAMILY COURTS

There is no unified code or set of procedures in the family courts in relation to the evidence of the young and the vulnerable. Reference has to be made to a disparate assortment of provisions. Much that is in use is borrowed from criminal practice and procedure. This pragmatic approach has led to difficulties with regard to funding and resources.

In 2010 the then President of the Family Division issued Guidance for Judges Meeting Children.[3] A central pillar of the Guidance was that any such meeting was not for the purpose of gathering evidence. The distinction between that process and the formal taking of evidence from a child has recently been emphasised by the Court of Appeal.[4]

Until 2010 the rule in family courts relating to the oral evidence of children was a presumption that they would not give oral evidence. The view of the Court of Appeal was "that it is undesirable that a child should have to give evidence in care proceedings and that particular justification will be required before that course is taken. There will be some cases in which it will be right to make an order. In my view, they will be rare".[5]

However, in 2010 the Supreme Court removed the presumption, making clear that a balanced decision was to be made in each case in which the issue arose.[6] The test was expressed by Baroness Hale in the following terms:

> When the court is considering whether a particular child should be called as a witness the court will have to weigh two considerations: the advantages that that will bring to the determination of the truth and the damage it may do the welfare of this or any other child. (para 24)

> ...the court must factor in what steps can be taken to improve the quality of the child's evidence and at the same time to decrease the risk of harm to the child. (para 27)

A referral made at that the time that this case was before the Court of Appeal led to the publication by the Family Justice Council of *'Guidelines: Children Giving Evidence In Family Proceedings'* (December 2011).[7] The Guidelines drew attention to a range of evidential matters that would

---

[3] Practice Note, April 2010, Guidelines for Judges Meeting Children who are Subject to Family Proceedings.
[4] See *Re KP (A Child)* [2014] EWCA Civ 554.
[5] *LM (By her Guardian) v Medway Council, RM and YM* [2007] 1 FLR 1698, per Smith LJ at para 44.
[6] *Re W (Children)(Abuse: Oral Evidence)* [2010] UKSC 12, [2010] 1 FLR 1485.
[7] [2012] 2 FLR 456.

assist in coming to a judgment as to whether or not oral evidence would be required. They also drew attention to the need to consider "the possibility of further questions being put to the child on an occasion distinct from the substantive hearing". Reference was also made to other "special measures" that might be deployed in order to assist the process of receiving oral evidence or the use of "intermediaries". Courts were pointed towards the guidance in criminal cases to be derived from the case of *R v Barker*[8].

The practice protocol for public law cases (the Public Law Outline – PLO) drew attention to the need to consider "special measures" and "provision for vulnerable witnesses" but without setting out any detail as to what these measures might be or how they would work. The Practice Direction in relation to Domestic Violence and Harm[9] refers to the "support" that the alleged victim or perpetrator may need in order to give evidence effectively but, again, provides no detail as to how this may be implemented.

The concepts of "special measures" and "intermediaries" are borrowed from criminal practice, but imported into family practice without the detailed statutory schemes that brought them into effect in criminal cases.

The Youth Justice and Criminal Evidence Act 1999 (YJCEA), sections 17 – 30 introduced a comprehensive scheme of special measures in order to protect the vulnerable in the criminal courts. Of particular interest is that section 28 has finally been dusted off in order to give new life to the original Pigot Committee recommendation in favour of the early video recording of the cross-examination of children. Pilot studies have been undertaken in three court centres in order to test the effectiveness of this way of proceeding. The outcome of these pilots is awaited.

The YJCEA was accompanied by guidance for the conduct of videotaped interviews of children, guidance that is now known as Achieving Best Evidence (ABE). Although designed for use in criminal proceedings, this guidance is often referred to in family proceedings where the taped interviews are produced.

The family courts have also borrowed from the criminal courts in the use of intermediaries.[10] Intermediaries were introduced in the criminal courts by section 29 of the YJCEA and are now known as Registered Intermediaries (RIs). They are provided by the Ministry of Justice. Intermediaries have been used in family cases but, as will be explored below, this can give rise to difficulties as to funding.

A particular difficulty that has vexed the family court is where an alleged perpetrator is to cross-examine, directly, the witness as to abuse.

---

[8] [2010] EWCA Crim 4.
[9] Family Procedure Rules 2010 (FPR 2010), PD12J.
[10] See *Re A (A Child)(Vulnerable Witness)(Fact Finding)* [2013] EWHC 2124 (Fam), [2013] 2 FLR 1473, Pauffley J and *Wiltshire County Council v N* [2013] EWHC 3502 (Fam), Baker J.

This may arise out of choice by the alleged perpetrator or, more likely, due to lack of funding for representation. Such a practice is prohibited by statute in the criminal courts. Legal assistance is provided to a defendant in such a situation.[11] There is no equivalent provision in the family court. At present there is no clear answer as to how judges should proceed when faced with such a situation. "Profound unease" has been expressed by a senior judge when faced with the prospect of the judge undertaking such an examination.[12]

The Practice Direction in relation to Domestic Violence and Harm recognises that "victims of violence are likely to find direct cross-examination by their alleged abuser frightening and intimidating, and thus it may be particularly appropriate for the judge or lay justices to conduct the questioning on behalf of the other party in these circumstances, in order to ensure both parties are able to give their best evidence". The solution proposed is that "the judge or lay justices should be prepared where necessary and appropriate to conduct the questioning of the witness on behalf of the parties, focusing on the key issues in the case".[13] As with so much of family practice in this area, this is a partial solution directed at a particular situation. It serves to illustrate the absence of a coherent, unified code for the common difficulties that arise.

Considerable additional assistance to the family practitioner is available from the Advocate's Gateway (TAG) Toolkit 13: Vulnerable Witnesses and Parties in the Family Courts. The Toolkit provides a comprehensive review of current arrangements together with a summary of materials that are of assistance from criminal proceedings. The Toolkit reminds advocates of their duties in dealing with the young and the vulnerable, in particular:

i. Advocates must establish at the earliest possible stage whether a client could be considered as vulnerable and ascertain the nature of the vulnerability.
ii. The advocate must also consider whether the client has the capacity to give instructions and competence to give evidence.
iii. The advocate must draw the court's attention to the client's vulnerability and begin the process of finding ways to assist the client in light of their vulnerability.
iv. Following from (iii), it is the duty of an advocate to decide whether to make a Part 25[14] application and instruct an expert in the

---

[11] Section 38(4) YJCEA and section 19(3)(e) of the Prosecution of Offenders Act 1985.
[12] *H v L and R* [2006] EWHC 3099 (Fam), [2007] 2 FLR 162 per Roderic Wood J at para 24. See also *Re B (A Child)(Private Law Fact Finding – unrepresented father)*, *D v K* [2014] EWHC 700 (Fam).
[13] PD12J para 28.
[14] FPR 2010, Part 25.

proceedings. An expert can assist by providing an opinion on the extent of the client's vulnerability and making recommendations about appropriate safeguards for that particular client.

The Toolkit also provides detailed guidance on Ground Rules Hearings. Whilst there is no formal requirement for such hearings in family proceedings, it is well recognised that if there is to be evidence from a young or vulnerable witness, such hearings are essential. The Toolkit provides a full checklist of matters that may be considered at such a hearing.

FUNDING ISSUES

In the criminal courts funding is in place, where necessary for the provision of special measures, intermediaries and cross-examination of victims. No such measures are available in the family courts. Judicial innovation has had some success.

Sir James Munby, the President of the Family Division, has confronted the funding gap by reference to the possibility of the Government, in the form of Her Majesty's Court and Tribunal Service (HMCTS), paying for the relevant services. A decision[15] that the funding of intermediaries in court should be paid for by HMCTS has survived a recent review by the Court of Appeal.[16] However, this leaves in dispute the issue of the funding of intermediaries for work done in supporting a litigant other than at court.

In another case the President proposed that it might be possible to call upon HMCTS to fund the representation of a party for the purpose of cross-examination of a victim of abuse.[17] This possibility was taken up by a trial judge in a different case. On 22nd May 2015 the Court of Appeal handed down a judgment reversing this decision (*Re K and H* – see footnote 16). The Court of Appeal proposed four means by which the objective may be achieved: (i) a direction that cross-examination could take place only subject to the condition that the alleged abuser was legally represented; (ii) questioning by the judge; (iii) questioning by a justices' clerk; (iv) the appointment of a Guardian for the children. However, the court recognised that there may be cases when none of these routes would secure the Convention rights of the relevant participants. Such cases may be those involving complex expert evidence or complex and/or confused factual evidence from a vulnerable witness. The court concluded that "in order to avoid the risk of a breach of the Convention, consideration should be

---

[15] *Re D (A Child)(No 2)* [2015] EWFC 2.
[16] *Re K and H (Children)* [2015] EWCA Civ 543 at para 40.
[17] *Q v Q* [2014] EWFC 31, [2015] 1 WLR 2040.

given to the enactment of a statutory provision for (i) the appointment of a legal representative to conduct the cross-examination and (ii) the payment out of central funds of such sums as appear to be reasonably necessary to cover the cost of the legal representative". Only time will tell whether the Government is willing to take up this clear invitation to make provision in family cases parallel to that already available in criminal cases.

THE FUTURE

In June 2014 the President of the Family Division set up a Working Group to report as to issues concerning vulnerable witnesses and children in the family courts. The group, headed by two Family Division judges, Hayden J and Russell J reported in February 2015. The recommendations of the group are broad ranging and comprehensive. They will lead to a coherent and codified set of arrangements for the receipt of and challenge to the evidence of the young and the vulnerable.

The recommendations of the group are built around amendments to the FPR 2010 and two new Practice Directions.

An addition to the overriding objective[18] is proposed. The court will "make provision for vulnerable parties and witnesses and children to assist them in improving the quality of their evidence and to participate fully in proceedings". The rules will be amended to direct that any party or witness in family proceedings must be considered to be entitled to assistance on the grounds of age, incapacity, fear or duress.

One Practice Direction will replace the 2010 Guidance for judges seeing children. It will set out in clear terms the status of the communication between the judge and child.

The second Practice Direction will make provision for the identification of vulnerable and intimidated witnesses and the arrangements that will need to be put in place to receive their evidence. The report specifically refers to the criminal pilot in relation to pre-recording evidence and anticipates that this will form part of the Practice Direction.

The report contains the following clear statement of intent: "Modernisation and reform must include the direct evidence of children and support for the evidence of children to be heard at the youngest age appropriate for each child; just as in the criminal court the Family Court should hear the evidence of children of pre-school age". The report anticipates that "this will ultimately require a substantial change in the prevailing culture in respect of the evidence of children on the part of

---

[18] FPR 2010 r1.1.

judges, social services, Cafcass and others who work with children in the family courts".

Other recommendations include:

i. Definition of the term 'vulnerable witness' should be extended to include intimidated witnesses (this is the case in criminal proceedings);
ii. There should be open days in the family courts to increase public awareness of the court, and allow members of the public and children/ young people to see what happens in the courts;
iii. There should be training for all family judges at all levels in seeing children;
iv. The PLO and Child Arrangements Programme should be amended to ensure that the procedure, practice and guidance for provision of special measures, support and/or assistance for vulnerable parties or witnesses, including children, to give their best evidence, should form part of the existing PDs where possible;
v. The rules and PDs should be drafted with reference to the existing 'Special Measures Directions In The Case of Vulnerable and Intimidated Witnesses" and the Criminal Procedure Rules for ground rules hearings;
vi. The PDs should specifically reference and approve the TAG toolkits, as already happens in criminal cases;
vii. The new rule and PDs and amendments to the existing PDs should be drafted by the Working Group in consultation with the Family Justice Council, Family Justice Young People's Board, the judiciary and the drafts sent for wider consultation to the Ministry of Justice and HMCTS;
viii. Particular consideration should be given to the provisions for parties and witnesses in cases of forced marriage and female genital mutilation who are likely to be vulnerable witnesses requiring support and special measures. This support should be provided by the Judge, court and advocates;

A further report from the Working Group is expected in July 2015.

CONCLUSIONS

In 1989 the stage was set for family proceedings to be in the vanguard of arrangements for receiving the testimony of children. That early opportunity was not taken up. The family courts now operate with a magpie collection of borrowed rules and disjointed practice directions and initiatives. There is a clear need for a radical overhaul.

In April 2014 the President of the Family Division described the arrival of the unified Family Court as a cultural revolution. The proposals of the Working Group carry that revolutionary spirit into the arena of vulnerable and young witnesses. No longer will the family courts borrow, piecemeal from criminal practice. The best of criminal practice will be taken and adapted to suit the Family Court. The proposed Practice Directions offer a comprehensive and coherent structure for the receipt of evidence from the most vulnerable.

No working group, not even a President, can conjure up funds for new initiatives. In *Re K and H* the Court of Appeal offered a clear invitation to the Government to supply funds for those hard cases where available practices cannot meet the Convention needs of the case. It is to be hoped that that challenge will be taken up and that the initiatives of the Working Group will be matched with the necessary funds.

USEFUL WEBSITE ADDRESSES:

The current ABE guidelines:
http://www.cps.gov.uk/publications/docs/best_evidence_in_criminal_proceedings.pdf

'Guidelines In Relation To Children Giving Evidence In Family Proceedings':
https://www.judiciary.gov.uk/wp-content/uploads/JCO/Documents/FJC/Publications/Children+Giving+Evidence+Guidelines+-+Final+Version.pdf

'Guidelines For Judges Meeting Children Who Are Subject To Family Proceedings':
http://www.fnf.org.uk/phocadownload/downloads/guidelines_for_judges_meeting_children.pdf

The Working Group Final Report (February 2015) and accompanying appendices:
https://www.judiciary.gov.uk/wp-content/uploads/2015/03/vwcwg-report-march-2015.pdf

Advocate's Gateway (and toolkits)
http://www.theadvocatesgateway.org/
http://www.theadvocatesgateway.org/toolkit

The Best Interests of the Accused and the Adversarial System

CONOR GILLESPIE
Barrister at Law

DOES THE ADVERSARIAL SYSTEM OPERATE AGAINST THE BEST INTERESTS OF A VULNERABLE DEFENDANT ?

Nature of the Adversarial System

The adversarial legal system operates a conflict based resolution to allegations where each side is responsible for the collection and presentation of its own evidence, where cross-examination is used as a means to comment upon the evidence, refute or discredit the prosecution case and aggressively battle for the accused.[1] The overriding objective is to deal with cases for the prosecution and defence fairly,[2] recognising the defendant's rights to a fair trial whilst respecting the interests of witnesses, victims and jurors3 as enshrined with Article 6 European Convention on Human Rights; Right to a fair trial.

Within adversarial trials the lawyers' main tool is advocacy which is the art of persuasion. It is the method by which lawyers conduct cases both by argument and by the manner of bringing out the evidence so as to convince the court or jury as the case maybe. The rationale underlying criminal jury trials is to allow for community standards and values of fairness and equity to be part of legal decisions through citizen participation.[4] It therefore

---

[1] John Hostettler, *Fighting for Justice: The History and Origins of the Adversarial Trial* (Waterside Press, 2006), 15 and 41.
[2] Crown Court Rules. Northern Ireland 1979. Available at https://www.courtsni.gov.uk/en-gb/publications/legislation/pageskdefault.aspx.
[3] Laura Hoyano, "Reforming the Adversarial Trial for Vulnerable Witnesses and Defendants ," *Criminal Law Review* (2014) (1): 4-29.
[4] Neil Vidmar, "Expert Evidence, the Adversary System and the Jury" *American Journal of Public Health* 95 (2005): 137-143.

The Best Interests of the Accused and the Adversarial System

cooperates with human nature because it works on the minds of the judge, the jury and the witnesses.[5]

If those witnesses are vulnerable by virtue of their age or some other reason, it is not too hard to imagine that they will have difficulty understanding their rights, coping with police interviews, giving evidence, understanding court proceedings and with decision making tasks6 let alone fully participating in the conduct of the case where argument is one of the main methods to persuade the jury as to the truth.

It is the Article 6(3)(d) ECHR[7] right which raises the greatest criticism of the adversarial system[8] along with the bundle of techniques and tactics which make up conventional cross examination,particularly with regards to children.[9]

Cross examination techniques have been shown to result in memory distortion in persons with Intellectual Disability (ID),[10] with repetition and option posing causing persons with ID to change their responses. This in turn detracts from their usefulness and credibility as witnesses. Similarly relevant answers may not be given because the vulnerable witness does not fully comprehend the questions put to them and may not readily seek clarification.[11]

Nevertheless, the prevailing view in this system is that a witness who gives a spontaneous and unconsidered answer to a question is more likely to be telling the truth in the most compelling way,i.e.best evidence, rather than one who has had the opportunity before hand to consider the issues and reflect on the subject matter.[12]

Therefore in order to challenge a witness in this manner the tactics deployed to utilise the different techniques of cross examination all too often led the Bar to engage in gladiatorial communication combat against the witness. This has led to an imbalance within the adversarial system and

[5] John Munkman, *The Technique of Advocacy* (Butterworths & Co 1991), 8.
[6] ILana Hepner, Mary N. Woodward and Jennet Stewart, "Giving the Vulnerable a Voice in the Criminal Justice System:The Use of Intermediaries With Individuals With Intellectual Disability," *Psychiatry, Psychology and Law*, (2014): accessed November 13, 2014, doi: 10.1080/13218719.2014.960032.
[7] 'to examine or have examined witnesses against him and to obtain the attendance and examination of witnesses on his behalf under the same conditions as witnesses against him'.
[8] Phillip Bowden, Terese Henning, & David Plater "Balancing Fairness to Victims: An Impossible Triangulation?," *Melbourne University Law Review* 37(2014): 539.
[9] Joyce Plotnikoff and Richard Woolfson. "Kicking and Screaming" ; The Slow Road to Best Evidence," in *Children and Cross Examination;Time to Change the Rules?*, ed. JR Spencer & Michael Lamb (Bloomsbury Publishing, 2012) 26-30.
[10] Mark R. Kebbell, Christopher Hatton and Shane D. Johnson, "Witnesses with Intellectual Disabilities in Court;what questions are asked and what influence do they have?," *Legal & Criminal Psychology* 9 (2004): 23-35.
[11] Annie Cossins "Cross Examination in Child Sexual Assault Trials; evidentiary safeguard or an opportunity to confuse?," *Melbourne University Law Review* 33(2009): 68-104.
[12] Ibid, at [3].

created unfairness against the witness as the barrister is communicatively adept in their natural environment whereas the witness is communicatively inept in an alien environment.

Nevertheless, the defence and the prosecution entitlement to challenge a witness's testimony remains a keystone to the essence of a fair trial, but under conditions most conducive to eliciting the truth in a process predicated upon equality of arms and effective participation. This is entirely consistent with the entitlement of all vulnerable participants to protection from further trauma.[13]

REBALANCING WITH THE USE OF SPECIAL MEASURES

In order to achieve this aim, these issues were first examined in an attempt to shift practitioners' perceptions to what is acceptable advocacy and rebalance the power differential within the court room away from gladiatorial combat and back to testing scrutiny of the evidence. An advisory group was set up to consider the use of video recordings as a means of taking evidence of children and vulnerable witnesses in criminal trials. Their recommendations, which followed a comprehensive examination of the criminal justice system, were delivered within the Pigott Report 1989.[14]

These recommendations resulted in the implementation of special measures legislation aimed at protecting the safety, physical and psychological well-being, dignity and privacy of victims and witnesses. The aim is to achieve best evidence, improving its quality in terms of completeness, coherence andaccuracy within the Criminal Justice Act 1991 and the Youth Justice and Criminal Evidence Act 1999. These special measures were wide ranging from the removal of wigs and gowns, to allowing pre-recorded cross examination, which is only now being piloted in England and Wales in three Crown Court locations, Liverpool, Leeds, Kingston Upon Thames by virtue of section 28 of the Youth Justice and Criminal Evidence Act 1999 ('YJCEA 1999').

In Northern Ireland comparative legislation exists under Criminal Evidence (Northern Ireland) Order 1999 though Article 16 (akin to section 28 of the YJCEA 1999) providing for video cross-examination of a witness has not been enacted even as a pilot scheme.

Internationally the need for special measures and for the protection of a witness from psychological harm is now recognised in The International Criminal Court by virtue of The Rome Statute 1998 Article 68: 'the Court

---

[13] Ibid, at [3].
[14] Advisory Group on Video-recorded Evidence, *Report of the Advisory Group on Video Evidence* (Home Office, 1989).

The Best Interests of the Accused and the Adversarial System

shall take appropriate measures to protect the safety, physical and psychological well-being, dignity and privacy of victims and witnesses'.[15]

For criminal trials the European Directive 2012/29 set 'Minimum Standards or rights, support and protection of victims of Crime' thus adding to the already established human rights enshrined with the United Nations Convention of Human Rights 1989. For children as witnesses there exists Article 3 of the United Nations Convention on the Rights of Children 1990 and the proposed European Child Directive 10065/14:2013/0408.

The effective implementation of condign special measures for vulnerable witnesses has been undoubtedly slow, nevertheless lawyers do recognise that it is not always about winning a case and have acknowledged the potential trauma that may be caused within the adversarial system. Lord Justice Hughes delivering the Hershman-Levy Memorial Lecture 2001 stated that 'it behoved us to be astute not to risk adding more abuse to any there may already have been, by requiring detailed questioning in semi public'. Baroness Hale in *Re W (children)*[16] succinctly expressed this sentiment when she stated, 'when the court is considering whether a particular child should be called as a witness, the court will have to weigh two considerations; the advantages that that will bring to the determination of the truth and the damage it may do to the welfare of this or any other child'.

The courts have recently begun to change attitudes towards the veracity of the evidence of vulnerable adult witnesses and children. The Lord Chief Justice in the English Court of Appeal in *R v Barker*[17] emphatically stated that 'children are as believable as adults'. The English Court of Appeal court has given guidance on the rules applicable to vulnerable witnesses, for example in *R v Lubemba*[18], *R v Jonas*[19], particularly through cross examination. The current position has been eruditely presented by Dr Emily Henderson in 'All the Proper Protections- The Court of Appeal Rewrites the Rules for the Cross-Examination of Vulnerable Witnesses'.[20]

Perhaps two of the most important initiatives in England were the Witness Intermediary Scheme (WIS) and The Advocate's Gateway (TAG). In 2013 The Advocacy Training Council launched TAG, a free

---

[15] 'In so doing, the Court shall have regard to all relevant factors, including age, gender as defined in article 7, paragraph 3 and health, and the nature of the crime, in particular, but not limited to, where the crime involves sexual or gender violence or violence against children. The Prosecutor shall take such measures particularly during the investigation and prosecution of such crimes. These measures shall not be prejudicial to or inconsistent with the rights of the accused and a fair and impartial trial'.
[16] [2010] UKSC 12.
[17] [2010] EWCA Crim 4 at [38] – [43].
[18] [2014] EWCA 2064.
[19] [2015] EWCA Crim 562.
[20] *Criminal Law Review Supplement. 60th Anniversary Issue* (2014). S29-S44.

website providing training resources and toolkits to help advocates identify vulnerable witnesses and defendants and to plan how to adjust their questioning incorporating ground rules that should be adopted for questioning within a trial relating to the particular vulnerabilities identified. These ground rules were based upon a written report on the witnesses communication difficulties derived from an assessment by a communication specialist, the Registered Intermediary (RI). The WIS came into effect with the first training in England in 2003 and helped witnesses early in 2004. The RI became a facilitator, transparently advising the police and courts on the witness's communication difficulties, whilst intervening in the event of miscommunication usually to advise the questioner how better to communicate with the witness. Those RIs trained were already communication specialists within their own profession, e.g. speech and language therapists, who then underwent a masters level equivalent training course in the law, practice and procedure.

The Registered Intermediary scheme pilot (NI) was launched in May 2013 for indictable offences in Belfast Crown Court, with 12 requests being made after 3 months. In November 2013 it was extended to all Crown Courts province wide and as of March 2014 there had been 106 requests for assistance with only 4 having been deemed as not eligible under the qualifying criteria. [21]

What is unique about the Northern Ireland scheme is that vulnerable defendants when giving evidence will be able to take advantage of the scheme.[22] However, the test criteria to qualify is differently expressed for vulnerable (prosecution) witnesses and defendants as it is 'their ability to effectively participate in proceedings', as opposed to being able to 'give their best evidence'.

The adversarial system is learning to change, adapt and become flexible as Lord Judge in his Bar Council Annual Law Lecture on 21 November 2013 stated 'the objective of the criminal trial is that justice should be done... it depends upon the proposition that the adversarial system will produce justice. But we have to face the reality that if the adversarial system does not produce justice, justice is to everyone involved in the process, it will have to be examined and it should be re-examined. If it fails to do so the system requires to be changed'.

However concerns and issues still remain for vulnerable defendants as a fair trial should not involve the abstract balancing between the rights

---

[21] Figures supplied by Department of Justice (NI) and the results evaluated in the Post Project Review, accessed February 7, 2015, https://www.dojni.gov.uk/publications/northern-ireland-registered-intermediaries-schemes-pilot-project.
[22] Article 21(B) of the 1999 order as inserted by Art 12 of the Justice Act (Northern Ireland) 2011, as amended by S.11 of the Criminal Justice Act (Northern Ireland) 2013.

claims of the defendant and the complainant and measures to protect one should not invariably detract from the rights of the other in a zero sum game.[23] It would seem that the balance has weighed against the vulnerable defendant.

VULNERABILITY DEFINITIONS

The adversarial system needs to adopt more inclusive definitions of vulnerability and classifications of the criteria for vulnerable witnesses both as children and adults for both prosecution witnesses, defendants and defence witnesses. Yet domestic legislation restrictively defines vulnerability for special measures within the CE(NI) O1999 Art 4(1)(a) and YJCEA 1999 s.16.[24]

A substantial number of defendants have conditions which cause them to have limited language ability and communication skills, learning disabilities, and to be acquiescent and suggestible; 16% of people placed in custody meet one or more of the assessment criteria for mental disorder[25] with a consensus of 50-60 % of young people who are involved in offending having speech, language and communication needs.[26]

Many individuals diagnosed with PTSD and ID will exhibit behavioural difficulties in areas such as concentration, communication, learning and memory abstract, thinking, planning or problem solving, social adaptive functioning such as maintaining eye contact, interpersonal skills, regulation of behaviour, academic ability, reading writing or understanding information.

If an individual presents without any formal label, diagnosis or certification it may well be the case (and generally is) that police officers, legal professionals and practitioners will be less likely to recognise, acknowledge or identify that individual as being vulnerable requiring assistance, despite exhibiting obvious and objective signs of vulnerability, as classed above. In other words if they do not have a significant impairment of intelligence and social functioning, according to the test criteria they are ineligible for assistance. Exhibited characteristics often go unnoticed, misconstrued or

---

[23] Laura Hoyano, "What is balanced on the Scales of Justice? In search of the essence of a fair trial," *Criminal Law Review* (2014) 4.
[24] Were the witness is eligible for assistance if they suffer from; (i) mental disorder or (ii) otherwise has a significant impairment of intelligence and social functioning; (b) that the witness has a physical disability or is suffering from a physical disorder.
[25] 'Criminal Justice Inspection Northern Ireland', accessed November 15, 2015, http://www.cjini.org/CJNI/files/e6/e684b2e9-231e-4c06-b496-5b744e10c0cb.pdfpara 3.18.
[26] Juliette Gregory and Karen Bryan. "Speech and language Therapy Intervention with Group of Persistent and Prolific Young Offenders in a Non- custodial Setting with Previously Undiagnosed Speech, Language and Communication Difficulties," *International Journal of Language and Communication Disorders* 46(2)(2011): 202-215.

simply ignored and thus the true nature and communication needs of the individual is not adequately or properly assessed.

However, what is of greater concern is that within the various police service guides, department of justice, public prosecutions victims charters and guides there is an insistence upon labelling an accuser as a victim pre-emptively before a verdict has been reached. Within the adversarial system there is a presumption of innocence and to term a participant as a victim, that is one who has suffered harm, implies that the act has already happened. This surely erodes that presumption and may engender a bias against an accused person thus prejudicing the outcome of the prosecution. That can never be fair and is not equality in the pursuit of justice.

What is equally disconcerting is the absence of the words accused/defendant within the police, government and prosecution literature when it references guides and prompts for the identification of vulnerability within a participant of the criminal justice system.

Quite rightly there have been strident moves to reduce the trauma suffered by prosecution witnesses as the result of gladiatorial cross examination and the resultant special measures and recent court of appeal decisions have refocused lawyers to a testing scrutiny of the evidence.

However, it would seem that the vulnerable defendant is playing catch up in not only being equally recognised but being equally protected from the initial stages of the investigationthrough to the testing of that allegation in court. The potential for bias can be seen in two defence case scenarios.

CASE A

Adult male defendant A appeared before the Crown court for 3 charges relating to possession and supply of Cocaine and cannabis and possession of unlicensed firearm. At trial a plea was entered to one count of being concerned in supply Class A, the others not being proceeded with. A received a 12 month custodial sentence. A declined legal representation and was assessed as being medically fit for interview, where his admissions formed the basis of the prosecution against him.

All the proper procedures were adhered to by the police within the search procedure with the police giving A the appropriate legal documents about the search and his rights.[27] On arrest and at the start of the interview A was cautioned and it appeared that A was treated in accordance with the codes of practice.[28]

---

[27] Such as a copy of the search warrant, s 20, Notice of Powers and Rights and s 1A, premises search record of the Police and Criminal Evidence Act (NI) 1989.
[28] 'you do not have to say anything, but I must caution you, you do not mention when questioned something which you later try to rely on in court you're your defence anything

A was isolated from his family during the search procedure in his parents home during the early evening and remained on his own throughout the late night booking in procedure at a police station far from his home were he was then informed that he was being held overnight and he would be interviewed in the morning. A declined legal representation. An important fact in the background of A is that he was sexually abused by a male teacher during primary school.

Interview format and language issues

The objectives of the investigation and interview as demonstrated by the format and language used by the police are to set in motion the official process of investigation, to advise the suspect of their rights and gather evidence. It is therefore a data driven rote exercise were the procedural objective is setting out the charges and the suspects rights by imparting legal concepts and definitions in compliance with the law, for example, the caution, the right to silence and self incrimination.

This procedure is not equipped to garner relevant information on the suspects communication understanding and abilities with the applicable definitions of vulnerability being too restrictive and outdated[29] excluding the more recently diagnosed hidden vulnerabilities which can affect the suspects effective participation. Defendants suffer the same issues and are equally deserving of the same protections as prosecution witnesses yet their is a clear lack of knowledge within police forces in this regard which is evident as there are none of the prompts, guidance and signposts to identify vulnerability in the suspect custody format as there are for prosecution witnesses within The Vulnerable and Intimidated Witnesses Guide; A Police Service Guide 2011; MOJ and PSNI.[30] Though there is some acknowledgement of the need for the protection of vulnerable defendants[31]

you do say may be given in evidence what the caution means to you is you don't have to speak to us, to me or my colleague at all during this interview. Ok. However should this matter go to court and you tell the court something which you haven't told me or my colleague the court can draw its own conclusion about how much you told us at the time. Ok'.

[29] Criminal Evidence Order (NI) 1999 Art 4, 'intelligence impairment and in social functioning and physical disability or disorder'.

[30] 'College of Policing, United Kingdom'. Accessed November 14, 2014, https://www.app.college.police.uk/app-content/investigations/victims-and-witnesses/ Part 2 defines vulnerability as 'intelligence impairment and in social functioning and physical disability or disorder'. Part 3.2.2 - 3.2.4 there are a series of prompts to help in the identification and assessment of vulnerability. It is a statutory obligation to assess the victim or other prosecution witnesses.

[31] 'Police Service of Northern Ireland Code of Ethics', Northern Ireland Policing Board accessed February 4, 2015, http://www.nipolicingboard.org.uk/final_code_of_ethics-2.pdf . ' to obtain evidence not by unfairness and oppression, not unreliable or self incriminating'.

it relies upon restrictive and outdated criteria which creates an imbalance against the suspect.

An objective analysis of the custody and interview records in Case A show that throughout this process there were ample signposts and prompts pointing towards his vulnerabilities for example, being addicted to methadone prescribed for heroin addiction, having been sexually abused as a young boy, having chronic obstructive pulmonary disease with 20% lung capacity, suffering mental health issues with depression and suicidal ideations.

Compounding the police inadequacies in recognizing vulnerabilities the medical tests for assessing medical fitness for interview and effective participation in court do not relate to signposting intellectual, cognitive or communication vulnerabilities to uncover true language ability, communication skills and learning disabilities, susceptibility to acquiescence / self incrimination and suggestibility. There are three main reason for this; firstly, the object of the initial medical questions are solely an assessment of fitness for interview but not an identification of vulnerabilities relating to communication issues. Secondly, there is no continual assessment duty, even when potential signposts arise in the interview. Thirdly, there is no provision in the format for follow up questions or prompts at any stage so it is a one time assessment with the Force Medical Officer who declares the suspect fit for interview. When there is no readily apparent change or deterioration in their medical condition this assessment remains for the whole remaining interview despite the objectively obvious communication issues which work against the best interests of the vulnerable detainee.

Linguistically this procedure also operates against the best interests of the suspect. The interview of A does provide for checks and balances within and for the evidential gathering process[32] and this interview process.[33] However the primary concern does not seem to be ensuring that the suspect actually has a clear and full understanding of the legal jeopardy he faces with the accusations. This seems to be a matter for the suspects solicitor to clarify and protect, however, whether one is present or not there is no provision for assessment and checking back that the suspect has actually understood the process and meaning of the caution and his rights. To comply with the codes of practice for police interviews it is sufficient to accept a confirmatory answer from the suspect in this situation with the language of the caution potentially effectively eroding the right to silence

---

[32] For example Criminal Procedure and Investigations Act 1996 Part II, pt 3.5; duty on the prosecuting authorities to investigate and assemble all relevant evidence whether that points to or away from the suspect.
[33] PACE (NI) 1989, Codes of Practice Code C.

as it can infer that if you don't talk now you will get into trouble when this goes to court.

Self incrimination as a legal concept is also another area of concern for the best interests of the suspect. Its true meaning over and above 'if you do say something it may be given in evidence' is not adequately explained and clarified especially when there is no clear explanation or understanding of the charges and what evidence can amount to proving them.

A later stated he didn't actually understand 'being concerned in the supply of class A', he believed he was just helping the police with their questions on his background and drug habits over the past years. He didn't grasp the significance of his self incriminations when accepting that he may have given friends drugs when he was getting some for himself which resulted in a conviction and jail sentence.[34]

Techniques and tactics within the interview process

The codes of practice do not specifically deal with the communication abilities of someone such as A. In A's case the police relied on argumentative cross examination tactics and techniques, for example 'I find it hard to believe...' and 'right lets cut to the chase, you've been beating about the bus', which would now be viewed as inappropriate comments in relation to vulnerable witnesses in court cross examination.

In 2014 interviews with A the police state they have texts messages sent to his mobile number from the mobile of a deceased girl who died of a heroin overdose March 2011 asking if A can get her cocaine, a time gap of 3 years. The police do not tell A there are no replies from his phone nor do they show him the text messages in written form but A nods his head and answers 'yeah' to assertions implying acceptance of getting friends drugs when he got them for himself. The police take this as acceptance of the assertion made. The police then later state to him, 'you have already accepted that you got drugs for your friends ' and then use that fact to extract further self incriminations from him.

Further to this, when asked about his arrest for possession of class A, the issue that arose with A was whether he was accepting that he was arrested

---

[34] Eileen Vizard. 'Common Vulnerabilities'. (paper presented at the Criminal Bar Association Conference. 'Vulnerable Defendants and Witnesses', Inner Temple, London 6 December 2014). ' The cognitive position of the vulnerable child or adult is that they do not understand concepts such as self incrimination and right to silence and may not have the IQ to realise that their answers could lead them to incriminate themselves, i.e. they lack cognitive strategies to sidestep questions or to see were the questions could lead and can give false positive answers, e.g. head nodding, yeah to stop the questioning or stressful situation. This is common with clinical interviews with adolescents who just want to get out of the room'.

for possession of class A or that he is accepting that he had possession of class A coke, i.e. self incrimination as the nature of the question used 'do you accept that now' was unclear as to what he was accepting yet the police asserted that he had in fact accepted possession of class A on this basis.

A number of reports were obtained on behalf of A. A psychologist report found A to be of average I.Q. and not overly suggestible nor acquiescent on assessment or from the police interview tapes. A Registered Intermediary trial report assessed A to be vulnerable and highlighted his communication difficulties, finding he was over compliant, acquiesced to confident questions, nods as acceptance to questions being made rather than his answer being yes to the allegation within the question and can be intimidated by males. None of which was identified within the fitness for interview assessment.

The importance in relation to A is that the RI report identified specific communication vulnerabilities, which it could be deduced are derived from a power differential of assertive authoritative males over him resulting from being abused by a male teacher. The RI report confirmed that he was intimidated by males and acquiesced to confident statements and was over compliant. The early engagement of an RI in interview could have picked up on the body language of A being in a submissive and intimidated manner and posture, preventing intimidating comments and flagged up the nature of the exchanges to make sure that A understood the nature of questions trying to elicit self incriminations in the context of the charges of being concerned in the supply of class A he was alleged to have committed.

Clearly A incriminated himself in his police interviews[35] and an application for the exclusion of evidence obtained within the interview is by the judge's discretion[36]. The procedure in Northern Ireland is that the judge listens to the interview tapes of A and assesses his performance within them. He considers any defence expert psychologists, psychiatrists opinion within a report based upon assessment of the suspects I.Q. and levels of suggestibility and acquiescence. The test being whether their existed oppression or unfairness and whether in all the circumstances it would be unfair to admit the evidence.

These tests, it is suggested are outdated as they do not take account of the more recently diagnosed hidden vulnerabilities. They do not allow for consideration of the best interests of the communication abilities of the suspect being potentially acted against as it is not objectively evident from the current format and assessment tests which does not breach the current rules.

---

[35] Criminal Justice Act 2003 and Criminal Justice (Evidence) (Northern Ireland) Order 2004.
[36] Police and Criminal Evidence Order 1989. Articles 74, unfairness and 76, judicial discretion.

The defendant is then presented with the choice to enter a plea and potential reduction of sentence or to gamble with going to trial on such an issue and gaining no credit for any sentence reduction if convicted. Not only do the police place an accused in such an invidious position the courts compound this by failing to recognise that the current exclusion test criteria is outdated and discriminatory against those vulnerable people who for various reasons are communicatively inept despite not qualifying as vulnerable within the current legislative parameters.

CASE B

B was a teenager accused of sexual assault. On hearing that an allegation had been made to the police the parents of the accused proactively contacted the police. They were however put in the position of having to plead with the police not to formally arrest B at home but allow B to attend at the police station voluntarily, as the parents knew the shock of being arrested at home would cause overwhelming trauma to him as he was an extremely vulnerable young teenager, who had ongoing serious medical conditions. The officer in the case had already taken the decision to arrest B at home and to then search the home for forensic evidence without any thought or consideration of the impact upon B and recanted only after the intervention of their solicitor allowing B to be brought to the police station for questioning where he was arrested for sexual assault. B remained silent throughout his interview as the interviewing officers did not conduct the best evidence interview of the complainant and therefore did not possess the full allegations of the complainant. They were not in a position to put the full detail of the case to B.

The police tactics of when and how to arrest and interview B from the moment the allegation is made arise the competing interests of the police to conduct an interview with the complainant, gather forensic evidence, arrest and interview B whilst realising B's human rights.[37]

Though the police interests won out, the tactic of arresting and interviewing B will not actually advance these interests as the interviewing officers did not have the complete allegations and had no specialist training or skills in dealing with children in interviews and any competent lawyer would surely advise their client to answer no comment in these circumstances.

An objective assessment by an RI in the balancing of these competing rights issues at this stage should conclude that B's rights should win out. B did not understand the legal concepts in the procedure or what charges

---

[37] United Nations Convention on the Rights of a Child 1989.

could be made against him without knowing specifically the allegations and his interview should not have taken place without an RI as his solicitor also had no specialist training or skills relating to vulnerabilities of this nature in these circumstances. Nor did the police seek any professional assistance from an RI to advise on communication with B.

The police actions operated against the best interests of B as his resultant no comment interview put him at risk of any subsequent court drawing an adverse inference from his interview silence.[38] What is unfair is that the burden to persuade the court not to draw the adverse inference is placed upon B[39] to show that his silence was not attributable to having no explanation or none that would stand up to scrutiny.[40]

The police, once again can act against the best interests of an accused person though within their rules of engagement. It is the accused person who must then shoulder the burden to satisfy the court that their resultant actions or inactions; in this case silence, should not be held against them.

RECOMMENDATIONS FOR MODERNISATION

In light of these issues I make the following recommendations to reduce the conflict based approach to the collection of evidence in favour of a more balanced approach were the vulnerable defendants best interests and rights are seen as equally important as those of the vulnerable prosecution witness;

Creation of an Legal Communication Passport- LCP. On any contact with a suspect or witness the LCP contains prompts and guidance to signposts of vulnerability and communication issues as standard good practice for a continual duty to assess and record the potential and actual impact upon and consequences to the best interests of that person.

Route to Court Communication Process- RCCP. Development of a planned route for a suspect when certain actions are taken, eg putting a charge, cautioning, it must be recorded that certain assessments have been undertaken and completed as prompted and guided within the LCP. This LCP and RCCP allow for the RI (if engaged) and the suspects defence team to know that the suspects best interests have been complied with and begin to form the blueprint, along with the RI report for their communication with the suspect for the preparation of their defence.

Communication Flying Squad- CFS when certain triggers have been positively identified as raising issues of vulnerability and communication concerns there is an on call or duty RI communication and legal team that

---

[38] Criminal Justice and Public Order Act 1994, Section 34.
[39] R v McGarry [1998] 3 All ER.
[40] R v Beckles [2005] 1 All ER 705.

can attend as swiftly as possible to aid in the communication vulnerability of the suspect.

Make it mandatory to have a lawyer and or RI properly qualified to act in the best interests of a vulnerable adult, when identified within the process as is proposed for children under Art 6, European Child Directive.

Audio/Visual recording of vulnerable suspect interviews.

Provision and funding for the RI and defence barrister to be instructed throughout the Magistrates Court Procedures. There is generally a long period within which the PPS consider the case papers and decide upon charges and the mode of trial. During this period it would be advantageous for the RI and defence team to work in completing the LCP, e.g. engaging expert witnesses such as psychologists. At arraignment all expert evidence issues will have been already engaged and hopefully completed thus alleviating the time pressures and constraints that exist at present reducing delay and allowing for a precise and realistic time frame for the setting down of the trial .

The early engagement of an RI in A and B would most likely have highlighted their vulnerabilities and communication issues. The applications of the above recommendations would better inform, guide and prompt the police to make appropriate decisions for and communicating effectively with clarity, checking back on understanding and without the spectre of intimidation preventing any manipulated self incrimination ensuring that the system operated in the best interests of the vulnerable defendant giving them the same safeguards and rights as vulnerable witnesses enjoy in the trial process.

Putting Theory Into Practice: A Comparison of the Guidance Available to Investigative Interviewers and Advocates when using Communication Aids in the Criminal Justice System

DR. MICHELLE MATTISON[1]
Lecturer in Psychology, Department of Psychology, University of Chester
Registered Intermediary

INTRODUCTION

Vulnerable people face numerous barriers in order to achieve equal access to justice. Some of these barriers relate to cognitive and psychological factors associated with the person's age or their developmental, social and intellectual functioning, while others relate to inappropriate criminal procedure practices.[2] To address these barriers, the Youth Justice and Criminal Evidence Act 1999 makes available a number of statutory special measures to assist vulnerable people in giving their best evidence.[3] Two of these special measures, section 29 'Examination through an Intermediary' and section 30 'Aids to Communication', directly provide provisions to enable vulnerable people's evidence to be as coherent, clear and accurate as

---

[1] The author would like to thank Professor Penny Cooper for her comments on an early draft of this work.
[2] Martine Powell, Michelle Mattison and Keith McVilly, "Guidelines for Interviewing People with Communication Impairment", Australian Police Journal 67, no. 2 (2013), 58.
[3] Sections 23 – 30 of the YJCEA 1999.

possible[4]. In practice, the role of an intermediary is to support the process of eliciting best evidence from witnesses in terms of seeking to avoid potential misunderstandings between parties.[5] For instance, section 29 states that an intermediary's function is: a) to communicate to the witness any questions put to them; b) to communicate to any persons asking such questions the answers given in reply and to explain such questions or answers so far as necessary to enable them to be understood by the witness or questioner.[6]

Indeed, "effective communication underlies the entire legal process: ensuring that everyone involved understands and is understood; otherwise the legal process will be impeded or derailed."[7] The special measures outlined in the YJCEA 1999 provide the foundations for effective communication to occur, and section 29 makes the function of an intermediary clear. In contrast, Section 30, Aids to Communication, is less clear.

Aids to Communication, in force from 2002, allows evidence to be given (whether by testimony in court or otherwise) through a device that the court considers appropriate, and which can be independently verified and understood:

> A special measures direction may provide for the witness, while giving evidence (whether by testimony in court or otherwise), to be provided with such a device as the court considers appropriate with a view to enabling questions or answers to be communicated to or by the witness despite any disability or disorder or other impairment which the witness has or suffers from.[8]

The case of *R v Watts*[9] is a momentous example of the Aids to Communication provision put into practice, and supports the notion that this special measure is one of the least contentious in the YJCEA 1999.[10] The four profoundly disabled witnesses in this particular case required devices to facilitate their usual means of communication in daily life, thus the process of giving evidence in court was appropriately adapted to their needs. Indeed, many witnesses with a 'disability or disorder or other impairment' use Alternative and Augmentative Communication (AAC).[11] AAC may include a low-tech or high-tech 'device', such as a computer,

---

[4] Victims and Witnesses Unit, "The Registered Intermediary Procedural Guidance Manual (London: Ministry of Justice, 2012), 9.
[5] Thelma Agnew, "Finding a Voice", Mental Health Practice, 9, no. 7 (2006), 10.
[6] Section 29 of the YJCEA 1999.
[7] Judicial College, "Equal Treatment Bench Book" (London, 2013), 12.
[8] Section 30 of the YJCEA 1999.
[9] *R v Watts* [2010] EWCA Crim 1824.
[10] Jonathan Doak and Claire McGourlay, Criminal Evidence in Context (London: Routledge, 2008), 47.
[11] Exact figures are not known.

voice synthesiser, symbol/alphabet board or book.[12] In such circumstances, every reasonable step should be taken to ensure that witnesses are supported in communicating via their usual means. In contrast, many people who are vulnerable (e.g., typically developing children, eligible for special measures under section 16 of the YJCEA 1999[13]) do not have a 'disability or disorder or impairment'[14], but they can, and have benefit from the use of an Aid to Communication during trial proceedings.[15] However, the amount of guidance available to practitioners concerning appropriate use of this special measure differs markedly between police officers and advocates.

CURRENT GUIDANCE FOR ADVOCATES

Advocates awareness of appropriate and inappropriate application of Aids to Communication is imperative, but until March 2015, this issue had sparely been addressed.[16] At present, Criminal Procedure Rules (CPR 2015) make reference to the use of Aids to Communication and state that "facilitating the participation of any person includes giving directions for the appropriate treatment and questioning of a witness or defendant, especially where the court directs that such questioning is to be conducted through an intermediary." and:

> (7) Where directions for appropriate treatment and questioning are required, the court must –
>
> (a) invite representations by the parties and by any intermediary; and
>
> (b) set ground rules for the conduct of the questioning, which rules may include—
>
> (i) a direction relieving a party of any duty to put that party's case to a witness or a defendant in its entirety,
>
> (ii) directions about the manner of questioning,

---

[12] Communication Matters, "About AAC," *Communication Matters*, (accessed on 24 August 2015), http://www.communicationmatters.org.uk/page/about-aac.
[13] Section 16 of the Youth Justice and Criminal Evidence Act 1999.
[14] Section 30 of the Youth Justice and Criminal Evidence Act 1999.
[15] Exact figures are not known.
[16] The Advocate's Gateway (a free online resource with advocacy guidance and training) launched a 'toolkit' on '*The use of communication aids in the criminal justice system*', which is discussed later in this article.

Putting Theory into Practice

(iii) directions about the duration of questioning,

(iv) if necessary, directions about the questions that may or may not be asked,

(v) where there is more than one defendant, the allocation among them of the topics about which a witness may be asked, and

(vi) directions about the use of models, plans, body maps or similar aids to help communicate a question or an answer. [17]

Here, communication aids are referred to as "models, plans, body maps or *similar aids* to help communicate a question or an answer."[18] Criminal Practice Directions (CPD 2013) also make reference to 'body maps':

In particular in a trial of a sexual offence, 'body maps' should be provided for the witness' use. If the witness needs to indicate a part of the body, the advocate should ask the witness to point to the relevant part on the body map. In sex cases, judges should not permit advocates to ask the witness to point to a part of the witness' own body. Similarly, photographs of the witness' body should not be shown around the court while the witness is giving evidence.[19]

With the exception of the aforementioned sections in CPR 2015 and CPD 2013, there is no further indication as to what an Aid to Communication may include. Section 30 of the YJCEA 1999 does not provide a definition either. Thus, by definition, or lack of, an Aid to Communication can encompass an unlimited spectrum of resources, ranging from a high-tech and bespoke computerised aid, to a humble pen and paper. In this instance, the Aids to Communication direction is the most loosely defined, ambiguous and flexible special measure available. This could be an advantage if advocates realise the scope for using Aids to Communication when planning to question vulnerable witnesses, but with so little attention paid to this subject in rules and guidance, it is doubtful that advocates are fully aware of the full potential.

In *R v Cokesix Lubemba; R v JP* [2014] EWCA Crim 2064, the Court of Appeal said: "It is now generally accepted that if justice is to be done to the

---

[17] Criminal Procedure Rules 2015 (SI 2015/1490) (L. 18) r.3.9 (6).
[18] Ibid.
[19] Practice Direction (CA (Crim Div): Criminal Proceedings: General Matters) [2013] EWCA Crim 1631; [2013] 1 W.L.R. 3164 (CPD) in particular at "General matters 3E.6: Ground rules Hearings to Plan the Questioning of a Vulnerable Witness or Defendant".

vulnerable witness and also to the accused, a radical departure from the traditional style of advocacy will be necessary. Advocates must adapt to the witness, not the other way round."[20] In this respect, it is important that advocates are not restricted to a closed definition or absolute list of what comprises an Aid to Communication – flexibility is essential. However, when applying for special measures, advocates are expected to: "explain why special measures would be likely to improve the quality of the witness' evidence."[21] The absence of any guidance for advocates about how Aids to Communication can improve the quality of the witness' evidence, potentially makes this task problematic. It could be that advocates only apply for this particular direction when they have sought advice from a Registered Intermediary following an assessment of a vulnerable witness' needs, but there are no research findings available to suggest this. The lack of information available for advocates on the use of Aids to Communication is surprising, especially when one considers the guidance that has long been available to police officers i.e., investigative interviewers.

CURRENT GUIDANCE FOR INVESTIGATIVE INTERVIEWERS

Since the publication of the Memorandum of Good Practice in 1992, investigative interviewers have been guided about the most effective and appropriate ways to use communication aids when questioning vulnerable witnesses.[22] Although this document dates back over 20 years, it makes very clear that "all props [i.e., communication aids] should be used with caution and without leading questions".[23] This recommendation still stands today and is clearly emphasised in Achieving Best Evidence (ABE 2011),[24] the contemporary police interviewing guidance document, however, this recommendation is absent from legislation, CPR 2015 and CPD 2013 despite the enrolment of Aids to Communication over a decade ago.

The advice that communication aids should be used with caution and without leading questions is based upon a wealth of laboratory research findings about the efficacy of communication aids when questioning vulnerable people.[25] Much of this evidence focuses upon the use of dolls, body outlines/maps and drawings (often referred to in the literature as

---

[20] *R v Cokesix Lubemba; R v JP* [2014] EWCA Crim 2064.
[21] Criminal Procedure Rules 2015 (SI 2015/1490) (L. 18) r.18.10 (b).
[22] Home Office, Memorandum of Good Practice, (Her Majesty's Stationary Office,1992).
[23] Ibid, 24.
[24] Achieving Best Evidence in Criminal Proceedings: Guidance on Interviewing Victims and Witnesses, and Guidance on Using Special Measures, (London: Ministry of Justice, 2011).
[25] Ibid.

Putting Theory into Practice

'props'), all of which have been tested in highly controlled experimental settings.[26] The purpose of such experiments is not only to further theoretical understanding of human memory and communication, but to inform investigative interviewers about the most effective (and ineffective) ways to gather and improve eyewitness testimony. ABE 2011 heavily draws upon the available empirical literature, and provides police officers with practical recommendations concerning appropriate use of communication aids.[27] CPR 2015 do not do this, and CPD 2013 only do this to a limited extent (the latter making reference to the use of 'body maps').[28]

ABE 2011 advises that communication aids can support and augment a person's recall of events, giving rise to some peoples enhanced competence to demonstrate what happened rather than explain in words alone.[29] Other advantages of communication aids are also highlighted, such as the provision of retrieval cues and memory triggers.[30] Importantly, it is also noted that if interviewers combine communication aids with appropriate questioning techniques, they can enable witnesses to recall their best evidence.[31] There are clear risks and pitfalls when communication aids are used inappropriately and when combined with leading or suggestive questioning – that is, their ability to confuse and even hinder communication. ABE clearly outlines these dangers.[32] The CPR 2015 and CPD 2013 do not provide advocates with any of this information.

Although some reference is made to trial proceedings, the main focus of ABE 2011 recommendations is on the questioning of vulnerable people during investigative interviews – not questioning in court.[33] Undeniably, there are clear differences in the purpose of an investigative interview and the purpose of examination by an advocate. However, the advantages, and importantly, the risks of using communication aids are highly relevant to advocates due to contrasting questioning styles adopted in investigative interviews and cross-examination.[34] For example, advocates, unlike police officers, are permitted to ask leading questions, and the vocabulary,

---

[26] Ibid, 89.
[27] Ibid, 89.
[28] Practice Direction (CA (Crim Div): Criminal Proceedings: General Matters) [2013] EWCA Crim 1631; [2013] 1 W.L.R. 3164 (CPD) in particular at "General matters 3E.6: Ground rules Hearings to Plan the Questioning of a Vulnerable Witness or Defendant".
[29] Achieving Best Evidence in Criminal Proceedings: Guidance on Interviewing Victims and Witnesses, and Guidance on Using Special Measures, (London: Ministry of Justice, 2011), 90.
[30] Ibid, 90.
[31] Ibid, 89.
[32] Ibid, 89.
[33] Ibid, 131.
[34] Rachel Zajac, Julien, Gross and Harlene Hayne "Asked and Answered: Questioning Children in the Courtroom." *Psychiatry, Psychology and Law,* 10 (2006): 199.

structure and sequence of questions is typically more complex.[35] The difference in questioning styles is likely to be a risk factor in the use of Aids to Communication in court settings, particularly in light of vulnerable people's increased susceptibility to leading or suggestive questioning.[36] While communication through an intermediary (section 29 of the YJCEA 1999) can address some of these issues, there are distinct differences between advocates' and intermediaries' perceptions of appropriate questions.[37] For instance, when asked to examine a list of questions, intermediaries, in comparison to advocates, have been found to identify a greater number of questions as leading.[38] This could have potential implications on the efficacy of Aids to Communication, particularly in cases where an intermediary is not appointed.

NEW GUIDANCE FOR ADVOCATES ON THE USE OF AIDS TO COMMUNICATION

The Advocate's Gateway (a free online resource that provides practical guidance to advocates working with vulnerable people) recently launched a 'toolkit' detailing appropriate and effective use of Aids to Communication in the criminal justice system – this is the first resource of its kind.[39] Developed by a working group comprising of academic researchers from the fields of psychology, law and policing and also, practitioners including Registered Intermediaries, an experienced practicing barrister (QC), and a member of the judiciary. Toolkit 14 draws upon relevant empirical evidence; the guidance set out in ABE 2011, and also, practitioner experience. Overall, Toolkit 14 provides advocates with informed recommendations about the most appropriate ways to use communications aids, and the risk associated with improper use.[40]

The toolkit begins by placing great emphasis upon supporting and facilitating communication with all vulnerable persons who come into contact with the criminal justice system (i.e., victims, witnesses and defendants). Advocates are advised from the outset about the overall benefits of using communication aids, namely, their ability to facilitate accurate, complete and coherent communication. Importantly, it is

---

[35] Ibid, 200
[36] Rachel Zajac and Harlene Hayne, "I Don't Think That's What *Really* Happened: The Effect of Cross-Examination on the Accuracy of Children's Reports." *Journal of Experimental Psychology*, 9, no. 3 (2003): 187.
[37] Sarah Krähenbühl, "Effective and Appropriate Communication with Children in Legal Proceedings According to Lawyers and Intermediaries." *Child Abuse Review*, 20 (2011): 407.
[38] Ibid, 407.
[39] Advocate's Gateway, Using Communication Aids in the Criminal Justice System (London: Advocacy Training Council, 2015).
[40] Ibid, 3.

highlighted that these benefits only arise when aids are combined with both *appropriate use* and *appropriate questioning*. Alike ABE 2011, Toolkit 14 thus informs advocates from the outset that there are clear risks and pitfalls when communication aids are used inappropriately and combined with leading or suggestive questioning – that is, their ability to confuse and even hinder communication.[41]

To minimise the risks associated with the use of Aids to Communication, Toolkit 14 outlines the importance of careful planning – something that is not detailed in CPR 2015 or CPD 2013.[42] Advocates are encouraged to carefully consider the following:

1. *Why* it necessary to use communication aids in their particular case;
2. *When* communication aids will be used (for example, pre-trial to aid preparation and/or during questioning);
3. *How* communication aids will be introduced and used.

In order facilitate effective and careful planning of Aids to Communication, it is recommended that advocates seek the assistance of a Registered Intermediary. An intermediary can assess the vulnerable person's communication needs *prior* to trial, and advise about the most effective means of communication.[43] Importantly, an intermediary can work with the vulnerable person to identify appropriate, neutral aids that are tailored to the witnesses' needs.[44] The findings of an intermediary assessment and recommendations about the use of Aids to Communication (if recommended) should be documented in the intermediary's report and the matter should be discussed during a 'Ground Rules Hearing'.[45]

As noted, the YJCEA 1999, CPR 2015 and CPD 2013 provide no clear definition about what constitutes an aid to communication, and rightly so. In order to take into account the subjective nature of each vulnerable person's communication needs, as well as the needs of each particular case (for example, the specific vocabulary required by the court), providing a single definition would be inappropriate at best, and somewhat restricting or unhelpful at worst. Toolkit 14 therefore takes an alternative approach and describes a number of commonly used communication aids, placing focus upon the particular *function* that these aids may serve.[46] Going beyond

---

[41] Ibid, 3, 6.
[42] Ibid, 4.
[43] Ibid, 4.
[44] Ibid, 5.
[45] Ministry of Justice, Registered Intermediary Procedural Guidance Manual (London: Home Office, 2012).
[46] Advocate's Gateway, Using Communication Aids in the Criminal Justice System (London: Advocacy Training Council, 2015), 6.

what is documented in current legislation, CPR 2015 and CPD, Toolkit 14, describes a number of communication aids that can:

i. allow evidence to be gathered, clarified or tested (e.g., dolls, figures and drawings);
ii. assist with psychological and physiological state management (e.g., prompt cards, break cards, emotion scales and calming objects);
iii. prepare vulnerable witnesses and defendants to give evidence and to establish the 'rules' of communications (e.g., a visual timetable).

Communication aids that can allow evidence to be gathered, clarified or tested

Items such as dolls, body diagrams, paper and pens have long been used by therapists, clinicians and teachers to bridge the gap between what children know and understand, and what they can express.[47] More specifically, these items have been found to scaffold children's reports by enabling them to (i) show and tell; (ii) communicate information that may be embarrassing; (iii) and/or to support memory retrieval.[48] Because of these benefits, investigators have long adopted their use in with vulnerable people in forensic settings.[49] Similarly, their use is also prevalent within court settings since the introduction of Registered Intermediaries, possibly giving rise to their reference in CPR 2015 and CPD 2013.[50] However, as noted, there are significant risks associated with inappropriate use of communication aids, and advocates should be mindful of them.

Dolls, figures and models

The use of anatomical dolls to support communication and recall with vulnerable witnesses, in particular, children, is perhaps the communication aid which has been subject to the most amount of research and debate. There is an overall consensus that anatomical dolls may provide a means of establishing the words that a vulnerable person uses for body parts, and they can allow for clarification of questions and answers, particularly in relation to matters concerning areas of touch that have *already* been

---

[47] Deborah Poole and Maggie Bruck, "Divining Testimony? The Impact of Interviewing Props on Children's Reports of Touching." *Developmental* Review, 32, (2012): 165.
[48] Ruth Marchant, "How Young is Too Young? The Evidence of Children Under 5 in the English Criminal Justice System." *Child Abuse Review*, 22, no. 6, (2013): 432.
[49] Deborah Poole and Maggie Bruck, "Divining Testimony? The Impact of Interviewing Props on Children's Reports of Touching." *Developmental* Review, 32, (2012): 165.
[50] Michelle Mattison, "Practitioners Perceptions and Use of Communication Aids in the Criminal Justice System." (PhD thesis, Lancaster University, 37–76).

Putting Theory into Practice

spontaneously reported.[51] However, findings from controlled laboratory studies are somewhat inconsistent about the positive effects on accuracy of recall when anatomical dolls are used to *initiate an account* and/or to *increase recall of new/additional details*.[52]

There is less debate and controversy surrounding the use of non-anatomically correct dolls (e.g., wooden artist dolls and pipe-cleaner figures), however, research is still not in complete agreement about the efficacy of these particular props, as some have yet to be empirically tested. Exercising their use with particular caution is advised.[53] For instance, dolls and figures should never be presented as items of play or be combined with leading/suggestive questioning techniques, as both factors can increase the likelihood of inaccurate information being produced.[54] ABE 2011 highlights this factor, yet CPR 2015 and CPD 2013 do not, despite 'models' being referred to in CPR 2015.[55] To illustrate the use of dolls, Toolkit 14 provides an example of a case where wooden artist dolls (with the assistance of a Registered Intermediary) were used *appropriately* in order to enable a deaf defendant to provide testimony of which he was unable to provide with sign-language alone:

> A deaf defendant was able to very successfully act out an action scene during his evidence/testimony. He used three wooden artist-type figures that are multi-jointed and a miniature bottle. He had initially attempted to describe the incident using sign language, but was unable to do so. The use of the figures enabled him to be animated and exact.[56]

Body diagrams and maps

Due to previous debate in the field of psychology surrounding the use of dolls, many practitioners began using body diagrams and maps as a

---

[51] Deirdre A. Brown, "The use of supplementary techniques in forensic interviews with children." *Children's testimony: A handbook of psychological research and forensic practice* (2011): 217-249.

[52] For a review, see: Deborah Poole and Maggie Bruck, "Divining Testimony? The Impact of Interviewing Props on Children's Reports of Touching." *Developmental* Review, 32, (2012): 165.

[53] Advocate's Gateway, Using Communication Aids in the Criminal Justice System (London: Advocacy Training Council, 2015).

[54] Deirdre A. Brown, "The use of supplementary techniques in forensic interviews with children." *Children's testimony: A handbook of psychological research and forensic practice* (2011): 217.

[55] Criminal Procedure Rules 2015 (SI 2015/1490) (L. 18) r.3.9 (6).

[56] Advocate's Gateway, Using Communication Aids in the Criminal Justice System (London: Advocacy Training Council, 2015), 7.

substitute.[57] These diagrams and maps are found in many different forms, for instance, some may be a simple, gender-neutral body outline. Others may be anatomically correct, clothed or unclothed. In forensic contexts, this communication aid is typically used in sexual offence cases to establish the words that a person uses for body parts.[58] Furthermore, the use of body maps is recommended in CPD 2013 for witnesses who need to indicate a part of the body.[59] In such cases, advocates are advised to "ask the witness to point to the relevant part on the body map, [and] judges should not permit advocates to ask the witness to point to a part of the witness' own body."[60] This is a sound direction, and in line with ABE 2011 recommendations regarding the questioning of vulnerable people in sex abuse cases.[61] However, empirical evidence for the effectiveness of body diagrams and maps is, as with dolls, somewhat mixed, and therefore, the same precautions and good practice guidance should apply when utilising this Aid to Communication. Again, while Toolkit 14 highlights the necessary precautions, CPR and CPD 2013 do not.

Writing and drawing

Writing and drawing are an Aid to Communication that is also frequently used by practitioners including investigative interviewers and Registered Intermediaries.[62] In contrast to the mixed empirical findings concerning the use of dolls and body diagrams, the benefits of using this tool to enhance eyewitness testimony have long been demonstrated with little contention. Moreover, asking witnesses (who have adequate literacy skills) to write their responses to questions on a blank piece of paper may be one of the most safe and reliable means of alternative communication for those who have difficulty providing responses to questions verbally. For example:

> In a case involving a young person who was a selective talker and unable to respond to questions asked by the interviewing officer,

---

[57] Deborah Poole and Maggie Bruck, "Divining Testimony? The Impact of Interviewing Props on Children's Reports of Touching." *Developmental* Review, 32, (2012): 165.
[58] Deirdre A. Brown, "The use of supplementary techniques in forensic interviews with children." *Children's testimony: A handbook of psychological research and forensic practice* (2011): 217.
[59] Practice Direction (CA (Crim Div): Criminal Proceedings: General Matters) [2013] EWCA Crim 1631; [2013] 1 W.L.R. 3164 (CPD) in particular at "General matters 3E.6: Ground rules Hearings to Plan the Questioning of a Vulnerable Witness or Defendant".
[60] Ibid.
[61] Achieving Best Evidence in Criminal Proceedings: Guidance on Interviewing Victims and Witnesses, and Guidance on Using Special Measures, (London: Ministry of Justice, 2011), 124.
[62] Michelle Mattison, "Practitioners Perceptions and Use of Communication Aids in the Criminal Justice System." (PhD thesis, Lancaster University, 37–76).

the young witness wrote in sentences on a piece of paper and the intermediary then read out her sentences, holding up the page for the camera to focus on. The case did not go to court but the alleged defendant was cautioned.[63]

In addition:

> Writing and drawing was used when working with an adult witness who had suffered a stroke, which had caused expressive difficulties/dysarthria (difficulty speaking caused by problems controlling the muscles used in speech). She was supported when giving her evidence by being able to write the words down. During the assessment it was important to assess her ability to accurately read and write words and sentences. She used her non-dominant hand to write, i.e. her left hand, as the stroke had caused a right-sided hemiplegia (paralysis). Her words were then read aloud by the intermediary who then checked with the witness that it was actually what she had wanted to say.[64]

In support of the use of drawing as an Aid to Communication, empirical studies have demonstrated that children who produce a drawing whilst recalling events, have been found to remember twice as much information than their peers who do not draw.[65] Importantly, drawing has also been shown to increase the accuracy of information produced when open questions are presented.[66] These positive effects have also been revealed with regard to emotionally-laden events[67] as well as for children who require additional, external support when retrieving memories (e.g., children with Autism Spectrum Disorder).[68]

As with the other communication aids described thus far, the empirical literature is clear that use of drawing has only revealed advantages when used in conjunction with appropriate, non-suggestive questioning (contrary to the traditional questioning styles adopted by advocates during

---

[63] Advocate's Gateway, Using Communication Aids in the Criminal Justice System (London: Advocacy Training Council, 2015), 9.
[64] Ibid, 9.
[65] Sarnia Butler, Julien Gross, and Harlene Hayne. "The effect of drawing on memory performance in young children." *Developmental Psychology* 31, no. 4 (1995): 597.
[66] Julien Gross and Harlene Hayne. "Drawing facilitates children's verbal reports after long delays." *Journal of Experimental Psychology: Applied* 5, no. 3 (1999): 265.
[67] Carmit Katz and Liat Hamama. ""Draw me everything that happened to you": Exploring children's drawings of sexual abuse." *Children and Youth Services Review* 35, no. 5 (2013): 877-882.
[68] Michelle L. A. Mattison, Coral J. Dando and Thomas C. Ormerod. "Sketching to Remember: Episodic Free Recall Task Support for Child Witnesses and Victims with Autism Spectrum Disorder." *Journal of autism and developmental disorders* 45, no. 6 (2014): 1751-1765.

cross-examination). When used in parallel with false events or suggestive questioning, an increase in the recall of erroneous information is observed.[69] Moreover, the importance of the vulnerable person himself/herself being the author of the drawing is imperative in order to ensure the picture is a salient and subjective representation. Production of drawings by anybody but the person being questioned (i.e., Registered Intermediaries; police officers; advocates), runs the risk of possibly contaminating the person's memory of events and/or inappropriately leading them.[70] Similarly, it is vital that the drawing has a concrete and stable identity in the person's mind – this can be tested simply by making a deliberate naming error (for example, asking "who is this?" and incorrectly saying a different name e.g., "So this is X?').[71] Again, while these recommendations have long been in cited in guidance for investigative interviewers, there is no such reference within CPR 2015 or CPD 2013, despite writing and drawing being one of the most reliable Aids to Communication.

Post-it notes and visual timelines

Many people's overall communication of events can be improved with the aforementioned aids, but some vulnerable people (e.g., very young children and people with Autism Spectrum Disorder) often have difficulty recalling particular aspects of events, namely, information that relates to categories such as location; date and time (referred to in the field of psychology as temporal information / source memory).[72] A number of creative methods are regularly used by Registered Intermediaries in the criminal justice process to support people in communicating temporal or source information.[73] For instance, post-it notes and visual timelines are suggested to assist vulnerable people in the sequencing of events, enabling aspects to be narrated chronologically.[74] They can be particularly useful in establishing whether an event took place before or after another, and are considered by practitioners to be especially effective in the case of multiple events. For example:

---

[69] Julien Gross, Harlene Hayne and A. Poole. "The use of drawing in interviews with children: A potential pitfall." *Focus on child psychology research* (2006): 119-144.
[70] Michelle Mattison, "Practitioners Perceptions and Use of Communication Aids in the Criminal Justice System." (PhD thesis, Lancaster University, 37–76).
[71] Ruth Marchant, "How Young is Too Young? The Evidence of Children Under 5 in the English Criminal Justice System." *Child Abuse Review,* 22, no. 6, (2013): 432.
[72] Dermot M. Bowler, Nicola J. Matthews and John M. Gardiner. "Asperger's syndrome and memory: Similarity to autism but not amnesia."*Neuropsychologia* 35, no. 1 (1997): 65-70.
[73] Michelle Mattison, "Practitioners Perceptions and Use of Communication Aids in the Criminal Justice System." (PhD thesis, Lancaster University, 37–76).
[74] Ibid.

> When working with a witness who offered comments describing events about an offence, the intermediary assisted the witness to create line drawings on post-it notes, representing each of the comments made. The witness then moved the post-its around so that she was able to retell the offence. Using this form of visual support in her narrative enabled the witness to focus on the order of events.[75]

Also:

> A defendant was supported by a timeline which was made using the chronology of events already stated, such as attendance at various primary schools, houses/moves, particular friends at certain times etc. The timeline was produced during the pre-trial meetings and brought to the ground rules hearing. The judge and counsel agreed to its use.[76]

Research is still in its infancy with regard to the best ways to support recall of temporal details in forensic settings, and to-date there are currently no findings from experimental studies that support the use of post-it notes and timelines. As with the other communication aids described so far, the strategies outlined should be adopted with caution; after very careful planning; and only applied with appropriate questioning techniques. Moreover, the use these techniques should only occur following assessment by a Registered Intermediary.[77] A Registered Intermediary should assess the vulnerable person's cognitive capacity and ability to conduct representational shift (understanding that the doll, figure, diagram or drawing is a representation of themselves or somebody else).[78]

Communication aids that can assist with state management

Coping with the unfamiliar and providing evidence in criminal proceedings can be a stressful and often frightening experience for many people. For vulnerable people, especially those who may be traumatised or have propensity for anxiety (such as people with learning disability and people with autism spectrum disorder), these feelings can be particularly prominent.[79] In addition, some people also have difficulty

---

[75] Advocate's Gateway, Using Communication Aids in the Criminal Justice System (London: Advocacy Training Council, 2015), 10.
[76] Ibid, 10.
[77] Ibid, 4.
[78] Ruth Marchant, "How Young is Too Young? The Evidence of Children Under 5 in the English Criminal Justice System." *Child Abuse Review*, 22, no. 6, (2013): 441.
[79] Brendan M. O'Mahony, "The emerging role of the Registered Intermediary with the vulnerable witness and offender: facilitating communication with the police and members

maintaining concentration for long periods of time, particularly when being questioned.[80] Thus, trauma, stress, anxiety and lack of concentration can negatively impact upon a person's ability to engage and communicate.

In any case concerning a vulnerable person, prearranged breaks from questioning should be considered prior to the start of proceedings (such as in a 'Ground Rules Hearing').[81] However, some vulnerable people may require additional breaks. Prearranged breaks can go some way in managing anxiety and stress, but supplementary techniques may also be required. For example, a number of communication aids are regularly used by Registered Intermediaries to address psychological and physiological state management, all of which can facilitate communication.[82] At present, empirical research on their efficacy and impact upon recall is minimal. Until data is available to support the use of the below Aids to Communication, their use should be exercised with caution, and only following assessment by a Registered Intermediary.

Prompt and symbol cards

To facilitate additional breaks, prompt and symbol cards typically containing text and/or symbols (e.g., 'break', 'stop' and 'toilet'), when laid out in front of the witness, can serve as a visual reminder that it is 'okay' to request a break.[83] For optimal effect, prompt and symbol cards should be tailored to the needs of the witness.[84] Some vulnerable people may not necessarily take the opportunity to have an additional break, and instead, wish to 'get it over with'. Nonetheless, transferring control of 'important things' to a vulnerable person can have overall positive effects on their emotional state, thus aiding their communication and recall.[85]

---

of the judiciary." *British Journal of Learning Disabilities* 38, no. 3 (2010): 232.

[80] Karen Saywitz and Lorinda Camparo. "Interviewing child witnesses: A developmental perspective." *Child Abuse & Neglect* 22, no. 8 (1998): 825.

[81] Advocacy Training Council, *Raising the Bar: the Handling of Vulnerable Witnesses, Victims and Defendants in Court* (London: ATC, 2011).

[82] Michelle Mattison, "Practitioners Perceptions and Use of Communication Aids in the Criminal Justice System." (PhD thesis, Lancaster University, 37–76).

[83] Advocate's Gateway, Using Communication Aids in the Criminal Justice System (London: Advocacy Training Council, 2015), 11.

[84] Ibid, 11.

[85] Ruth Marchant, "How Young is Too Young? The Evidence of Children Under 5 in the English Criminal Justice System." *Child Abuse Review,* 22, no. 6, (2013): 437.

Putting Theory into Practice

Feelings and emotions scales

A pictorial 'feelings' or 'emotions scale' can be used to monitor stress and anxiety experienced during proceedings and/or questioning.[86] As with prompt cards, it is good practice for the scale to be in front of the person so that they can communicate where they are on the scale at regular intervals. A Registered Intermediary can facilitate the use of a scale, and if the person reaches a certain point, a break should be considered. Importantly, scales should be tailor-made during a Registered Intermediary's assessment to ensure that they have subjective meaning.[87] Toolkit 14 provides a clear example of how this communication aid was used with a vulnerable defendant who had Autism Spectrum Disorder:

> A defendant with autism was helped by a routine in which he expressed his emotions by using a pictorial 'emotions thermometer'. The thermometer had a gauge with calm/relax at the bottom and worried/rage/frustrated at the top. A central column (made of red card) was movable and the defendant was able to express his emotions using this while in the dock and in the witness box. This simple routine enabled him to externalise his feelings and assisted his emotional containment.[88]

Calming objects

Quiet, calming objects that can be 'fiddled' with (e.g., blu-tack and stress balls) are an additional communication aid that can help to monitor and manage stress and anxiety, whilst also maintaining concentration during interviews, cross-examination or trial proceedings. It is important that a balance is struck between using calming objects to manage anxiety and maintain concentration, and not allowing them to distract the witness or become objects of play.[89]

Communication aids that can help prepare witnesses to give evidence

Many vulnerable people have no prior knowledge or understanding of the criminal justice system. Consequently, coping with the unknown,

---

[86] Advocate's Gateway, Using Communication Aids in the Criminal Justice System (London: Advocacy Training Council, 2015), 12.
[87] Ibid, 12.
[88] Ibid, 13.
[89] Deirdre A. Brown, "The use of supplementary techniques in forensic interviews with children." *Children's testimony: A handbook of psychological research and forensic practice* (2011): 217.

disruption to regular routines, and being placed in unfamiliar settings with unfamiliar people can cause significant anxiety and impact upon communication.[90] Despite these factors being pertinent to vulnerable witness testimony, there is no reference in CPR 2015 and CPD 2013. However, it is possible to address anxiety with the use of visual timetables, prompt and symbol cards.[91]

Visual timetables

Visual timetables contain text and/or pictures that represent a series of events in time, such as the order of proceedings (useful for vulnerable defendants), or simply an outline of what will happen when a witness arrives at court.[92] The purpose of this communication aid is to enable a vulnerable person to predict *what* will happen and *when*, and should of course, be tailored to the witness' or defendant's particular needs as well as the case itself. For instance:

> A defendant with autism was greatly helped by knowing exactly where he was in the trial. A pictorial and written order of the trial was made with simple explanations of each phase, i.e., jury swearing in; opening speech; evidence in chief; cross-examination etc. He was able to tick off on a side column when each stage had finished. The intermediary liaised with the barristers in order to keep the timetable accurate.[93]

Rules and other prompt cards

Akin to preparing witnesses and defendants about what will happen and when, it is also important that time is taken to establish and reinforce the 'rules' of communication.[94] Interactions with authority figures in forensic settings differ greatly from the interactions that many vulnerable people are accustomed to.[95] For instance, many children do not realise that

---

[90] Ray Bull, "The investigative interviewing of children and other vulnerable witnesses: Psychological research and working/professional practice." *Legal and Criminological Psychology* 15, no. 1 (2010): 5-23.
[91] Advocate's Gateway, Using Communication Aids in the Criminal Justice System (London: Advocacy Training Council, 2015), 14.
[92] Ibid, 14.
[93] Ibid, 15.
[94] Ruth Marchant, "How Young is Too Young? The Evidence of Children Under 5 in the English Criminal Justice System." *Child Abuse Review*, 22, no. 6, (2013): 439.
[95] Thomas D. Lyon, "Assessing the competency of child witnesses: Best practice informed by psychology and law." In *Children's Testimony: A Handbook of Psychological Research and Forensic Practice* (2011), 69-85.

interviewers/questioners are naïve to their experiences of the event in question, and assume that interviewers/questioners know the answers, or worse, know more than them.[96] Indeed, findings from empirical research have long documented the effect that authority figures can have on vulnerable people's responses to questions.[97] Therefore, clear explanation of the 'rules' of communication should be explained, and prompt cards with symbols and/or text can be utilised to assist vulnerable people in learning and remembering the 'rules' (such as 'Say if you don't understand', 'Tell me if I get it wrong', 'No guessing'.[98] Importantly, this communication aid should be first introduced during an intermediary assessment and made available during questioning to help the person remember the 'rules'.[99] Further, it is essential that the 'rules', their wording, and their presentation are adapted to the needs of the vulnerable person.[100]

CONCLUSIONS

The special measures outlined in the YJCEA 1999 provide sound foundations for courts to treat and question vulnerable witnesses appropriately, paving the way for effective communication to be achieved, so long as these special measures are utilised effectively. Despite these legislative provisions, focussed on enabling vulnerable witness testimony at court, there is a clear imbalance between the guidance available to police officers and advocates about appropriate use of Aids to Communication. The guidance available for advocates is somewhat sparse and it is dispersed amongst rules and practice directions. Further, previous research has suggested that practitioners, who question vulnerable people in court settings, are largely unaware of the findings from empirical studies about the effects of appropriate and inappropriate questioning.[101] In contrast, police offices are provided with detailed guidance (in the form of ABE 2011) and training is available to them.

---

[96] Karen Saywitz, Lynn Snyder, and Vivian Lamphear. "Helping children tell what happened: A follow-up study of the narrative elaboration procedure." *Child Maltreatment* 1, no. 3 (1996): 200.
[97] Rachel Zajac and Harlene Hayne. "I don't think that's what really happened: The effect of cross-examination on the accuracy of children's reports." *Journal of Experimental Psychology: Applied* 9, no. 3 (2003): 187.
[98] Advocate's Gateway, Using Communication Aids in the Criminal Justice System (London: Advocacy Training Council, 2015), 12.
[99] Ibid, 11.
[100] Ruth Marchant, "How Young is Too Young? The Evidence of Children Under 5 in the English Criminal Justice System." *Child Abuse Review*, 22, no. 6, (2013): 439.
[101] Ray Bull, "The investigative interviewing of children and other vulnerable witnesses: Psychological research and working/professional practice." *Legal and Criminological Psychology* 15, no. 1 (2010): 5-23.

It is not suggested that guidance and training alone is sufficient. It is clear that police interviewing practices still demonstrate great need for improvement because best practice recommendations are not followed to the extent that they should be.[102] Nonetheless, it is somewhat bemusing that police officers are provided with a detailed national guidance document about 'achieving best evidence' (and for them to undergo specialist training on the subject prior to conducting interviews) only for these key principles to be omitted from guidance concerning the later stages of criminal procedure. The overriding message about the use of communication aids is that they can improve witnesses' testimony, but they must be used with caution. Advocates need to be made aware of this, and theory should be transferred into practice guidance accordingly.

The provision for Registered Intermediaries may go some way in facilitating the transfer of theory into good practice knowledge between criminal procedure stages, but is this enough? For instance, the current version of the Registered Intermediary Procedural Guidance Manual (RIPGM 2012) does not provide intermediaries with information about the benefits and risks of using communication aids, however, the manual recommends that intermediaries should include in their reports "what, if any, communication aids should be used (for example symbols, charts, pictures, etc) and how they should be used."[103] It is important to bear in mind that intermediaries are appointed for their expertise in facilitating communication. It is unwise to assume that *all* intermediaries will be aware of the empirical evidence concerning the risks of inappropriate use of Aids to Communication. Toolkit 14 should therefore prove valuable to intermediaries as well as advocates, and should be referenced in the next revision of the RIPGM.

Since its introduction, the Advocate's Gateway has made great strides in providing advocates with a wealth of resources about the best ways to question vulnerable people in court. The resources that the Advocate's Gateway provide, bring together for the first time, legislation, case law, rules, directions, and importantly, empirical research. Moreover, the Advocate's Gateway website has been endorsed by CPD (2013); *R v Lubemba* (2014), and the Leveson report (2015), which should give rise to advocate's being more aware of the resources at their disposal. Indeed, the publication of Toolkit 14 draws attention to the effective use of Aids to Communication, but could more be done? CPD 2013 makes reference to the use of body maps for sexual offence cases, but directions regarding other

---

[102] Criminal Justice Joint Inspection, "*Achieving best evidence in child sexual abuse cases: A joint inspection.*" (London: HMCPSI Publications, 2014).
[103] Ministry of Justice, "The Registered Intermediary Procedural Guidance Manual (London: Home Office, 2012), 38.

Aids to Communication are not stated. CPR 2015, while listing a number of Aids to Communication, provides no further information on their use. At the very least, what should be noted, are the known risks associated with inappropriate use of Aids to Communication. Consideration should be given as to how this issue could be addressed.

There is a wealth of research relating to the use of communication aids in forensic i.e., police interview settings. To some degree, the findings from this research can be translated into court settings given that focus is upon the questioning of vulnerable people for evidential purposes. However, it would be more appropriate for laboratory research to take a direct approach and to establish the efficacy of props when vulnerable people provide evidence via live link or indeed in the courtroom itself. Similarly, field research into the use and application of Aids to Communication in court (e.g., court observations; case file and transcript reviews), are other possible lines of enquiry that would inform understanding and practical application of section 30. Such research would help to expand guidance, rules and practice directions. Training for advocates on Aids to Communication would also be better informed with further research, and thus theory may be better translated into practice.

BIBLIOGRAPHY

Advocate's Gateway, *Using Communication Aids in the Criminal Justice System*. London: Advocacy Training Council, 2015.

Advocacy Training Council, *Raising the Bar: The Handling of Vulnerable Witnesses, Victims and Defendants in Court*, London: ATC, 2011.

Agnew, Thelma, "Finding a Voice", Mental Health Practice, 9, no. 7 (2006): 10-11.

Association of Chief Police Officers (ACPO). (2009). *National investigative interviewing strategy*. Bedfordshire, UK: National Policing Improvement Agency.

Barlow, Claire M., Jolley, Richard P., White, David G and Galbraith, David. "Rigidity in children's drawings and its relation with representational change." *Journal of experimental child psychology* 86, no. 2 (2003): 124-152.

Bjorklund, David. *Children's thinking: Cognitive development and individual differences*. Pacific Grove, CA: Brooks/Cole, 2005.

Bowler, Dermot M., Matthews, Nicola J and Gardiner, John M, "Asperger's syndrome and memory: Similarity to autism but not amnesia."*Neuropsychologia* 35, no. 1 (1997): 65-70.

Brown, Deirdre A, "The use of supplementary techniques in forensic interviews with children." *Children's testimony: A handbook of psychological research and forensic practice* (2011): 217-249.

Bull, Ray, "The investigative interviewing of children and other vulnerable witnesses: Psychological research and working/professional practice." *Legal and Criminological Psychology* 15, no. 1 (2010): 5-23.

Burton, Mandy, Roger Evans, and Andrew Sanders, *Are Special Measures for Vulnerable and Intimidated Witnesses Working? Evidence from the Criminal Justice Agencies.* London: Home Office, 2006.

Burton, Mandy, Roger Evans, and Andrew Sanders, "Vulnerable and intimidated witnesses and the adversarial process in England and Wales." *International Journal of Evidence and Proof* 11, no. 1 (2007): 1-23.

Butler, Sarnia, Gross, Julien and Hayne, Harlene. "The effect of drawing on memory performance in young children." *Developmental Psychology* 31, no. 4 (1995): 597-608.

Chae, Yoojin. "Application of laboratory research on eyewitness testimony." Journal of Forensic Psychology Practice, 10, no. 3 (2010): 252-261.

Charles, Corrine, "Special Measures for Vulnerable and Intimidated Witnesses: Research Exploring the Decisions and Actions Taken by Prosecutors in a Sample of CPS Case Files. London: CPS, 2012.

Communication Matters, "About AAC," *Communication Matters*, (accessed on 24 August 2015), http://www.communicationmatters.org.uk/page/about-aac.

Cooper, Penny, Backen, Paula and Marchant, Ruth, "Getting to Grips with Ground Rules Hearings: A Checklist for Judges, Advocates and Intermediaries to Promote the Fair Treatment of Vulnerable People in Court" *Criminal Law Review*, 6 (2015): 420-435.

Criminal Justice Joint Inspection, *"Achieving best evidence in child sexual abuse cases: A joint inspection."* (London: HMCPSI Publications, 2014).

Criminal Procedure Rules 2015 (SI 2015/1490) (L. 18) r.3.9 (6).

Davies, Graham M., Westcott, Helen L and Horan, Noreen. "The impact of questioning style on the content of investigative interviews with suspected child sexual abuse victims." *Psychology, Crime and Law* 6, no. 2 (2000): 81-97.

Dickinson, Jason J., Poole, Debra A and Bruck, Maggie. "Back to the future: A comment on the use of anatomical dolls in forensic interviews." *Journal of Forensic Psychology Practice* 5, no. 1 (2005): 63-74.

Doak. Jonathan and McGourlay, Claire, *Criminal Evidence in Context.* London: Routledge, 2008.

Drummey, Anna B and Newcombe, Nora S. "Developmental changes in source memory." *Developmental Science* 5, no. 4 (2002): 502-513.

Gee, Susan and Pipe, Margaret-Ellen. "Helping children to remember: The influence of object cues on children's accounts of a real event." *Developmental Psychology* 31, no. 5 (1995): 746.

Goodman, Gail S and Melinder, Annika. "Child witness research and forensic interviews of young children: A review." *Legal and Criminological Psychology* 12, no. 1 (2007): 1-19.

Goodman, Gail S., Quas, Jodi A., Batterman-Faunce, Jennifer M., Riddlesberger, M. M and Kuhn, Jerald. "Predictors of accurate and inaccurate memories of traumatic events experienced in childhood." *Consciousness and Cognition* 3, no. 3 (1994): 269-294.

Gross, Julien and Hayne, Harlene, "Drawing facilitates children's verbal reports after long delays." *Journal of Experimental Psychology: Applied* 5, no. 3 (1999): 265-283.

Gross, Julien, Hayne, Harlene and Poole, A. "The use of drawing in interviews with children: A potential pitfall." *Focus on child psychology research* (2006): 119-144.

Henderson, Emily, "All the proper protections - the Court of Appeal rewrites the rules for the cross-examination of vulnerable witnesses", *Criminal Law Review*, 2 (2014): 93-108

Home Office, *Memorandum of Good Practice on Video Recorded Interviews with Child Witnesses for Criminal Proceedings*, London: Her Majesty's Stationary Office, 1992.

Judicial College, *Equal Treatment Bench Book*. London, 2013.

Katz, Carmit and Hamama, Liat, "Draw me everything that happened to you": Exploring children's drawings of sexual abuse." *Children and Youth Services Review* 35, no. 5 (2013): 877-882.

Krähenbühl, Sarah, "Effective and Appropriate Communication with Children in Legal Proceedings According to Lawyers and Intermediaries." *Child Abuse Review*, 20 (2011): 407-420.

Larsson, Anneli S., and Michael E. Lamb. "Making the most of information-gathering interviews with children." *Infant and Child Development*, 18, no.1 (2009): 1-16.

Marchant, Ruth, "How Young is Too Young? The Evidence of Children Under 5 in the English Criminal Justice System." *Child Abuse Review*, 22, no. 6, (2013): 432–445.

Marchant, Ruth and Page, Marcus, "Bridging the gap: Investigating the abuse of children with multiple disabilities." *Child Abuse Review* 1, no. 3 (1992): 179-183.

Mattison, Michelle, "Practitioners Perceptions and Use of Communication Aids in the Criminal Justice System.", PhD thesis, Lancaster University, 2015, 37–76.

Mattison, Michelle L. A., Dando, Coral J and Ormerod, Thomas C, "Sketching to Remember: Episodic Free Recall Task Support for Child Witnesses and Victims with Autism Spectrum Disorder." *Journal of autism and developmental disorders* 45, no. 6 (2014): 1751-1765.

Milne, Rebecca, and Ray Bull. "Interviewing witnesses with learning disabilities for legal purposes." *British Journal of Learning Disabilities* 29, no. 3 (2001): 93-97.

Milne, Rebecca and Bull, Ray. "Interviewing victims of crime, including children and people with intellectual disabilities." *Practical psychology for forensic investigations and prosecutions* (2006): 7-24.

Ministry of Justice, *Achieving Best Evidence in Criminal Proceedings: Guidance on Interviewing Victims and Witnesses, and Guidance on Using Special Measures.* London: Home Office, 2011.

Ministry of Justice, *Registered Intermediary Procedural Guidance Manual.* London: Home Office, 2012.

Lyon, Thomas D, "Assessing the competency of child witnesses: Best practice informed by psychology and law." In *Children's Testimony: A Handbook of Psychological Research and Forensic Practice* (2011), 69-85.

O'Mahony, Brendan M, "The emerging role of the Registered Intermediary with the vulnerable witness and offender: facilitating communication with the police and members of the judiciary." *British Journal of Learning Disabilities* 38, no. 3 (2010): 232-237.

Pipe, Margaret-Ellen, Lamb, Michael E., Orbach, Yael and Esplin, Phillip W., "Recent research on children's testimony about experienced and witnessed events." *Developmental Review* 24, no. 4 (2004): 440-468.

Pipe, Margaret and Salmon, Karen, "Dolls, drawing, body diagrams, and other props: Role of props in investigative interviews." *The evaluation of child sexual abuse allegations: A comprehensive guide to assessment and testimony* (2009): 365-395.

Plotnikoff, Joyce and Woolfson, Richard, "Making best use of the intermediary special measure at trial." *Criminal Law Review*, 2, (2008): 91–104.

Poole, Deborah and Bruck, Maggie, "Divining Testimony? The Impact of Interviewing Props on Children's Reports of Touching." *Developmental Review*, 32, (2012): 165-180.

Poole, Debra Ann, and Jason J. Dickinson. "Evidence supporting restrictions on uses of body diagrams in forensic interviews." *Child abuse & neglect* 35, no. 9 (2011): 659-669.

Powell, Martine, Mattison, Michelle and McVilly, Keith, "Guidelines for Interviewing People with Communication Impairment", Australian Police Journal **67**, no. 2 (2013), 58-63.

Practice Direction (CA (Crim Div): Criminal Proceedings: General Matters) [2013] EWCA Crim 1631; [2013] 1 W.L.R. 3164 (CPD).

R v Cokesix, Lubemba; R v JP [2014] EWCA Crim 2064.

R v Watts [2010] EWCA Crim 1824.

Saywitz, Karen and Camparo, Lorinda, "Interviewing child witnesses: A developmental perspective." *Child Abuse & Neglect* 22, no. 8 (1998): 825-843.

Saywitz, Karen, Snyder, Lynn and Lamphear, Vivian. "Helping children tell what happened: A follow-up study of the narrative elaboration procedure." *Child Maltreatment* 1, no. 3 (1996): 200-212.

Smith, Kevin and Tilney, Steve, *Vulnerable adult and child witnesses*. Oxford: Oxford University Press, 2007.

Teoh, Yee-San, Yang, Pei-Jung, Lamb, Michael and Larsson, Annelie, "Do Human Figure Drawings Help Alleged Victims of Sexual Abuse Provide Elaborate and Clear Accounts of Physical Contact with Alleged Perpetrators?", *Applied Cognitive Psychology*, 24 (2010): 287-300.

Youth Justice and Criminal Evidence Act 1999.

Zajac, Rachel, Gross, Julien and Hayne, Harlene, "Asked and Answered: Questioning Children in the Courtroom." *Psychiatry, Psychology and Law*, 10 (2006): 199-209.

Zajac, Rachel and Hayne, Harlene, "I don't think that's what really happened: The effect of cross-examination on the accuracy of children's reports." *Journal of Experimental Psychology: Applied* 9, no. 3 (2003): 187.

Vulnerable Voices?

JENNY TALBOT OBE[1], WAINE CLEGG AND
ANTHONY FLETCHER[2]
Prison Reform Trust and the Working for Justice Group

INTRODUCTION

Anthony and Waine have learning disabilities. Both have direct experience of the criminal justice system, including time spent in prison. They are members of the Working for Justice Group, which works to raise awareness of people with learning disabilities caught up in the criminal justice system, drawing attention to the difficulties they encounter and promoting positive change. Group members work as co-trainers, running learning disability awareness training for criminal justice staff; are consulted on 'translating' information into Easy Read[3], and have worked closely with the Criminal Cases Review Commission[4] to help develop a suite of Easy Read materials; and regularly speak at events, such as the first international event of the Advocacy Training Council and The Advocate's Gateway, 'Addressing Vulnerability in Justice Systems', which considered the proper treatment of vulnerable witnesses, suspects and defendants.

EXPERIENCES OF THE CRIMINAL JUSTICE SYSTEM

Anthony describes his experience of the criminal justice system as 'scary', which he attributes to having a learning disability. He found it hard to understand what was happening to him in court because, he says, everything happened 'so fast', adding that the judge spoke 'gibberish' and used 'long words I had never heard of in my life'. When asked about his experience of being a defendant, Waine said:

> When I was up before the magistrates and crown courts it was daunting for me. I didn't know what to expect. I tried to listen

[1] See End Notes, Box 1.
[2] See End Notes, Box 2.
[3] See End Notes, Box 3.
[4] See End Notes, Box 4.

to what was being said but just stared into thin air. The solicitor was a different one to the one who actually came to speak to me back in my cell. I felt confused when listening to some of the words that were being told to the judges. I couldn't wait to get out of the court and back in my cell. I was asked if I understood what was happening and I just said 'yes', even though it wasn't very clear to me. I just accepted everything going on around me and couldn't wait for it to end.

Waine says he made 'good use' of his time while in prison and completed a motor mechanics course, with the help of the tutor. When he left prison, however, he found it hard trying to find a proper home and the help he needed to 'stop going back'.

VULNERABILITY AND SUPPORT NEEDS

Anthony is at pains to point out that people with a learning disability aren't born vulnerable, but like anyone else need support at particular times in their life. Many people with a learning disability find new situations, such as appearing in court, especially hard to deal with. The physical environment can be intimidating and the language used is often complex with a vocabulary not generally encountered on a daily basis. Waine adds that just because a person has a learning disability, 'it doesn't mean we can't do things'. For example, in addition to effective public speaking skills and working as co-trainers, Waine is good at DIY and computers, while Anthony volunteers as a carer in an old people's home.

RECOGNISING SUPPORT NEEDS

High numbers of people with support needs come into contact with criminal justice services on a daily basis (see, for example, Talbot, 2012[5] and Department of Health, 2009[6]). While some people's support needs will be known about in advance, others may be unaware of their condition or choose not to disclose information. There are a number of reasons why people may not ask for help, including embarrassment, fear of ridicule or a more punitive response should their condition be made known.

On the whole, criminal justice staff are not good at recognising when an individual might have a learning disability or other support need. It

---

[5] Talbot, J. (2012) Fair Access to Justice? Support for vulnerable defendants in the criminal courts. London: Prison Reform Trust.
[6] Department of Health (2009) The Bradley Report: Lord Bradley's Review of people with mental health problems or learning disabilities in the criminal justice system. London: Department of Health.

is hoped that routine screening will soon be introduced by a new service called 'liaison and diversion'.[7] Subject to approval by HM Treasury in autumn 2015, liaison and diversion services will be made available in every police custody suite and criminal court in England by 2017. Qualified health personnel will screen and, where appropriate, assess suspects and defendants for a range of conditions and support needs. Their assessments will help to inform criminal justice decision making, including what support or reasonable adjustments are necessary to ensure an individual's effective participation in court proceedings.

MEETING SUPPORT NEEDS

Anthony and Waine think that criminal justice staff, defence lawyers, and members of the judiciary need a better understanding of the kinds of support that people with learning disabilities need. Small changes in the way things are done can make a big difference. For example, making information available in Easy Read, not using jargon, giving people extra thinking time, and asking in a kindly way whether people might need help. Although everyone involved in the criminal justice process can help to make a positive difference, sometimes specialist help will be needed. Specialist help can be provided in court through, for example, an intermediary.[8]

Extensive guidance is available on how vulnerable defendants should be supported in court; see for example, The Advocate's Gateway Toolkits,[9] the Equal Treatment Bench Book,[10] Criminal Practice Directions,[11] and the online resource, *Mental health, autism & learning disabilities in the criminal courts*.[12]

Support for vulnerable defendants is not an optional extra – the Equality Act 2010 strengthened and harmonised anti-discrimination law and created important new duties and rights. Reasonable adjustments, as required by the Equality Act, help to ensure that individuals such as Anthony and Waine are better able to participate effectively in court proceedings and enjoy fair access to justice.

---

[7] See End Notes, Box 5.
[8] See End Notes, Box 6.
[9] See End Notes, Box 7.
[10] See End Notes, Box 8.
[11] See End Notes, Box 9.
[12] See End Notes, Box 10.

Box 1:

Jenny Talbot OBE is director of *Care not Custody* at the Prison Reform Trust and chair of the National Appropriate Adult Network, Waine Clegg and Anthony Fletcher are members of the Working for Justice Group

The Prison Reform Trust is an independent charity that works to create a just, humane and effective penal system. We do this by inquiring into the workings of the system; informing prisoners, staff and the wider public; and by influencing Parliament, government, and officials towards reform: http://www.prisonreformtrust.org.uk The Prison Reform Trust has published a number of reports, and made recommendations, concerning people with learning disabilities and difficulties caught up in the criminal justice system, see No One Knows: http://www.prisonreformtrust.org.uk/nok

National Appropriate Adult Network: whenever police detain or interview an adult who they suspect may be 'mentally disordered or otherwise mentally vulnerable', they must secure an appropriate adult (AA). This includes, but is not limited to, people with mental ill health, learning disabilities or autistic spectrum conditions.

The AA's role is to protect the rights and welfare of the suspect, ensuring that they are able to participate equally and effectively in the process. The key responsibilities of the role, as defined in the Police and Criminal Evidence Act 1984 Codes of Practice, are:

- To support, advise and assist the person while in detention and/or during any interview
- To protect the person's rights, ensuring that they understand and can exercise them
- To observe and inform the police if they are not acting properly, fairly and with respect for the rights of the person
- To facilitate communication between the person and the police.

For further information, see http://www.appropriateadult.org.uk

Box 2:

Waine Clegg and Anthony Fletcher are members of the Working for Justice Group. The Working for Justice Group is a group of individuals with a learning disability who have direct experience of the criminal justice system as suspects, defendants, offenders and prisoners. They work to raise awareness of people with learning disabilities in the criminal justice system and to promote positive change. The group is supported by KeyRing Living Support Networks, with the Prison Reform Trust. For further information, including free learning disability awareness training for criminal justice professionals and practitioners, contact hugh.asher@keyring.org

KeyRing Living Support Networks provide independent living support enabling individuals with learning disabilities, and other needs, to live independently in the community. Support is based on people (network members) living in their own homes but sharing their skills and talents with each other and with their communities. KeyRing believes that community connections are important, and encourages network members to make good links with others in their neighbourhood. Network members have campaigned for street lights, run neighbourhood improvement schemes and saved lives: http://www.keyring.org/home

Box 3:

Easy Read documents present information using simple words and pictures making it easier to read and to understand. Easy Read can help people with reading comprehension difficulties, including people with learning disabilities, learning difficulties and also people for whom English is not their first language. Easy Read is a reasonable adjustment that can help to ensure equal access to information for people with reading and comprehension difficulties. Examples of Easy Read can be found at http://www.keyring.org/cjs-easyread

See also: Am I making myself clear? Mencaps's guidelines for accessible writing: https://www.mencap.org.uk/node/6040

Box 4:

The Criminal Cases Review Commission is the independent public body set up to investigate possible miscarriages of justice in England, Wales and Northern Ireland: http://www.ccrc.gov.uk/ The Commission has worked extensively with the Working for Justice Group to develop accessible information, including an Easy Read application form and related guidance: http://www.ccrc.gov.uk/making-application/how-to-apply/

Box 5:

Liaison and diversion is a process whereby people of all ages with mental health problems, learning disabilities, substance misuse problems or other vulnerabilities are identified and assessed as early as possible as they pass through the criminal justice system. Following screening and assessment, individuals are given access to appropriate services including, but not limited to, mental health and learning disability services, social care, and substance misuse treatment.

Information from liaison and diversion assessments is shared appropriately with relevant agencies so that informed decisions can be made, for example, about charging, case management, sentencing and diversion. Diversion may occur within the youth and criminal justice system or away from it, for example, into treatment and care (NHS England, 2014: Liaison and Diversion Operating Model 2013/14).

Liaison and diversion services will be made available in police custody suites and the criminal courts across England by 2017, subject to a successful business case and Ministerial approval. For further information, see http://www.england.nhs.uk/commissioning/health-just/liaison-and-diversion/

Similar services, referred to as criminal justice liaison services, exist in Wales.

Vulnerable Voices

> **Box 6:**
>
> The role of an intermediary is to facilitate two-way communication between the individual with communication support needs and other participants in the legal process, and to ensure their communication is as complete, accurate and coherent as possible. Intermediaries can assist the courts in meeting their obligations to ensure that a defendant is able to participate effectively in court proceedings. For example, intermediaries can assess a defendant's communication skills; help them to follow court proceedings, the course of a trial and the case against them; and assist prosecutors, defence solicitors and barristers rephrase questions that the defendant does not understand, and help to communicate their answers to the court.
>
> Although defendants are excluded from special measures provisions, including that of an intermediary, the court has inherent powers to take such steps as are necessary to ensure that a defendant is able to participate effectively in court proceedings and, should a case come to trial, has a fair trial; and this includes the appointment of an intermediary.
>
> For further information, see The Advocate's Gateway, Toolkit 16: http://www.theadvocatesgateway.org/images/toolkits/16intermediariesstepbystep060315.pdf

> **Box 7:**
>
> The Advocate's Gateway gives free access to practical, evidence-based guidance on vulnerable witnesses and defendants; it is hosted by the Advocacy Training Council: http://www.theadvocatesgateway.org

> **Box 8:**
>
> The Judicial College's Equal Treatment Bench Book, a guide for judges, magistrates and all other judicial office holders, was revised and updated in November 2013:
>
> https://www.judiciary.gov.uk/publications/equal-treatment-bench-book/
>
> The Courts and Tribunals Judiciary website notes that 'Although aspects of the guidance may seem familiar, and some of its general principles are well-known, the messages it contains are worth reiterating. Fair treatment is a fundamental principle embedded in the judicial oath, and it is therefore a vital judicial responsibility. Treating people fairly requires awareness and understanding of their different circumstances, so that there can be effective communication and so that steps can be taken, where appropriate, to redress any inequality arising from difference or disadvantage. This [guidance] covers some of the important aspects of fair treatment about which we should all be aware. It also makes some suggestions as to steps that judges may wish to take, in different situations, to ensure that there is fairness for all those involved in the justice process.'
>
> There are three sections of particular relevance:
>
> - Mental disabilities, specific learning difficulties and mental capacity: https://www.judiciary.gov.uk/wp-content/uploads/JCO/Documents/judicial-college/ETBB_Mental_disability_2013+_finalised_.pdf
> - Children and vulnerable adults https://www.judiciary.gov.uk/wp-content/uploads/JCO/Documents/judicial-college/ETBB_Children_Vulnerable_adults+_finalised_.pdf
> - Social exclusion and poverty: https://www.judiciary.gov.uk/wp-content/uploads/JCO/Documents/judicial-college/ETBB_Social_Exclusion__finalised_.pdf

Box 9:

The Courts and Tribunals Judiciary website notes that 'The Criminal Practice Directions were wholly revised and updated in October 2013 with the principle aim of making them more accessible to practitioners as well as encapsulating both legislative change and best practice. They were further updated last July [2014] and this represents the third amendment. The amended version will come into effect from 6th April 2015':

https://www.judiciary.gov.uk/publications/criminal-practice-directions-amendment-no-3-effective-from-6-april-2015/

There are four sections of particular relevance:

- 3D Vulnerable people in the Courts
- 3E Ground rules hearings to plan the questioning of a vulnerable witness or Defendant
- 3F Intermediaries
- 3G Vulnerable defendants, and these can be found at: https://www.judiciary.gov.uk/wp-content/uploads/2015/03/crim-pd-consolidated-with-amendment-3-edited1.pdf

Box 10:

Developed by Rethink Mental Illness and the Prison Reform Trust, Mental health, autism & learning disabilities in the criminal courts is a free online resource for magistrates, district judges and court staff. It includes information about different conditions, and how vulnerable defendants can be supported in court; film clips include individuals with learning disabilities or mental health conditions talking about their experiences in court: http://www.mhldcc.org.uk/

A Postscript

It has been a great pleasure to host at the Old Bailey several training days for new intermediaries. The structure of their day here has usually begun with a short greeting and then the group is then split into two to observe a couple of ongoing trials and then to observe a mock session involving an intermediary at work.

What follows by way of a postscript to this excellent current publication is by way of a short extension to the introductory talk that I give which itself was inspired by a conversation with the Recorder of London, Judge Hilliard QC.

I usually begin the training day with a short history of the Old Bailey itself and its role both in the City of London and in the delivery of criminal justice. That history, fascinating as it is, has no place here. What is of importance to stress here, is how the work of the intermediary fits in to the present day criminal justice system. Quite simply, for us it is now an integral part of the long process whereby justice is done. Perhaps it is worth considering, just for a moment, the great distance we have travelled in the development of that process.

Trial by ordeal was an ancient judicial practice whereby the guilt or innocence of the accused was determined by subjecting them to sometimes highly dangerous even life threatening experiences. The test was one of life or death and the proof of innocence was survival. The accused was considered to be innocent if they escaped injury or if their injuries healed. In medieval Europe, trial by ordeal, like trial by combat, was considered to be a procedure based on the idea that God would help the innocent by performing a miracle on their behalf. The ordeal stood alongside the taking of an oath and the account of witnesses, as the route by which a verdict was to be reached. What ordeals there were; for example, by fire, by boiling water or by being submerged in cold water three times. If that was the accused's fate, he or she was considered to be innocent if they floated and considered to be guilty if they sank. 1215 saw not only the signing of Magna Carta but also the end of priestly cooperation in trials by fire and water, they being forbidden by Pope Innocent. So ended in effect the notion that the stronger and more able bodied won their cases regardless of its merit and so began the decline of the use of techniques that had nothing whatever to do with justice but simply took into account the physical strength or resilience of the accused.

As things have developed there has been a growing and developing recognition of the position of victims and witnesses. We have reached the position now where all of us who toil in the field of the criminal justice system appreciate and understand that victims and witnesses are conscripts and not volunteers. There has been a paradigm shift in the way we approach their participation and I am confident that in the view of the vast majority of my colleagues a significant contribution to that process has been made by the introduction of the intermediary into the process.

The statute defines their purpose as being to "improve the quality of the evidence". Ground rules, special measures, written questions in advance of the trial and so on have all passed into our daily vocabulary to the point where the position reached by most if not all of the judiciary seems to be "why would I not want the help that all this can give me in my management of this case?" What was at the outset I am sure something of a judicial lion's den for the first wave of intermediaries has now hopefully become, no doubt with some rare exceptions, something much less hostile and much more welcoming.

Due in no small part to the pioneering, persistent and courageous work of a few the role of the intermediary in the appropriate case has become an essential part of the delivery of a fair trial. They and their work are valued and necessary.

This book represents the first extremely successful International Conference *Addressing Vulnerability in Justice Systems* hosted by the Advocacy Training Council in June this year. I commend the superb breadth of professionals who shared their expertise, and who have contributed to this publication.

The important work of The Advocate's Gateway, and the recognition of a multidisciplinary approach when working with vulnerable people will help to ensure fairer access to, and participation in, justice systems for the most vulnerable in our society.

HHJ Michael Topolski QC
December 2015